Oneida Carlisle Indian School Immortals

Native American Sports Heroes Series
Volume III

Oneida Carlisle Indian School Immortals

Tom Benjey

Carlisle, Pennsylvania

Carlisle, Pennsylvania

Copyright 2025 © Tom Benjey

Published by Tuxedo Press
Carlisle, PA 17015
TuxedoPress.com

First printing, 2025

All rights reserved. No part of this publication may be reproduced, stored in a retrieval system, or transmitted, in any form or by any means, electronic, mechanical, photocopying, recording, or otherwise, without the prior permission of Tuxedo Press.

ISBN 978-1-936161-09-6
Library of Congress Control Number

Contents

	Preface	vii
	Introduction	1
1	Chauncey Archiquette	17
2	Charles Baird	31
3	Wilson Charles	37
4	Casper Cornelius	53
5	Joel Cornelius	57
6	Phillip Cornelius	61
7	Samson Cornelius	65
8	Wallace Denny	69
9	Benjamin Doxtator	93
10	David George	97
11	Levi E. Hill	101
12	Louis Island	107
13	Emerson Metoxen	115
14	James Metoxen	137
15	Jonas Metoxen	141
16	Job J. Moore	153
17	Amos Reed	159
18	Caleb Sickles	163
19	Benjamin Skenandore	179
20	Fred Skenandore	183
21	Thomas A. Skenandore	189
22	Lewis Webster	193
23	Hugh & Joel Wheelock	197

Contents (cont'd)

24	Martin Wheelock	209
25	Other Oneidas	217
	Appendices	
A	Toughness	221
B	Players with Years Played	229
	Illustrations	231

Preface

Writing about people born in the 19th century presents problems for researchers. Births weren't always recorded and censuses and tribal rolls weren't always consistent or accurate. Fortunately, Wisconsin marriage records can now be found online. While they don't include dates of birth for either the bride or groom, they have the names of both parents for each of them. Knowing parents' names is very helpful.

A problem researching Carlisle Indian School football players is identifying who exactly was on the varsity. In my prior book, *Gridiron Gypsies: How the Carlisle Indians Shaped Modern Football*, I perused newspaper coverage for Carlisle's games, school publications, and their opponents' school newspapers and yearbooks to find players' names mentioned. A total of 500 young men were on Carlisle's varsity but many of them seldom, if ever, got into a varsity game. Those young men were relegated to the Second or Third Team games to get playing time. Sadly, those games received scant coverage from newspapers and school publications.

Most students played on the intramural teams. The various shops, debating clubs, and even the band fielded teams. Experienced varsity players gained coaching valuable experience tutoring these players. Those games rarely received coverage, even in the school newspaper.

One often reads about a person who claimed to have played alongside Jim Thorpe. Quick checks of when the person was at Carlisle usually debunks these claims as Jim Thorpe only played on the 1907, 1908, 1911, and 1912 teams. He wasn't even on campus during the 1909 and 1910 seasons. It's no wonder people wanted to be associated with the Carlisle Indians. They were a great team and are legendary because of how well they played the game.

Oneidas played key roles on the Carlisle team from the beginning in 1893 through the end in 1917 and would have if the 1918 season had been played as it was scheduled. Oneidas were integral to Carlisle's success.

Introduction

Richard Henry Pratt (seated), Susan Longstreth, Spotted Tail. In rear: Mary Anna Longstreth, Rebecca Haines

In order to fully appreciate what the young men who played football at Carlisle Indian School accomplished, one needs to know more about the school itself and how it came to be created. Having that knowledge as a foundation, why and how the football team came into being and why it was so successful will make more sense. Let's start with the founding of Carlisle Indian Industrial School.

Origin of the School

The Carlisle Indian football team was unlike any that came before or since. It was the product of the school, its superintendent, the coach, and the players themselves. Carlisle Indian School would not have existed had it not been for a special man having radical beliefs and the conviction to act on them. At eighteen, he apprenticed himself to a tinsmith and worked at that trade for three years until the Confederates shelled Fort Sumter.

Eight days later, he enlisted in the 9th Indiana Regiment. When his three-month enlistment expired, he re-enlisted, this time as a sergeant in the 2nd Regiment Indiana Cavalry. Among other places, he fought at Chickamauga. On April 12, 1864, he was commissioned as a 1st lieutenant in the 11th Indiana Cavalry. The hostilities over, Richard Henry Pratt mustered out on May 29, 1865. He and Anna Laura Mason, whom he had married in 1864 while home on a recruiting trip, returned to Logansport, Indiana to operate a hardware store. But that didn't work out. So, Pratt returned to military life as a 2nd lieutenant with brevet ranks of 1st lieutenant and captain for meritorious service during the Civil War. Assigned to the 10th United States Cavalry, he led a newly formed unit of African-American enlisted men with white officers. The Indians they were fighting dubbed the troops "Buffalo Soldiers" because of the perceived similarity of the soldiers' hair with bison fur. Although quickly promoted to 1st lieutenant, further promotions were a long time in coming. However, he was often addressed or referred to as Captain Pratt to honor his brevet rank.

In 1875, Lt. Pratt was assigned the task of transporting seventy-two Cheyenne, Kiowa, Comanche, Arapaho, and Caddo Indian prisoners taken in the Red River War to Fort Marion (renamed Castillo de San Marcos) in St. Augustine, Florida and served as their jailer. Most of the prisoners were men, but the group included one Cheyenne woman prisoner—Buffalo Calf Woman, the wife of Medicine Water—who had killed a farmer. Also transported were a number of wives and children who had refused to be separated from their husbands and fathers. Eleven of the Comanche and Kiowa prisoners were actually Mexican captives who had been raised as tribal members.

After eight years of working directly with Indian scouts and former slaves as soldiers, Pratt developed a philosophy that guided him the rest of his days. He believed that all Indians and African-Americans needed to compete on equal terms with whites were: "The rights of citizenship include[ing] fraternity and equal privilege for development." Equal opportunity for Indians became the great crusade of his life.

Pratt used the Fort Marion incarceration as a laboratory to demonstrate that wild Indians could be converted into peaceful, enlightened citizens. He immediately replaced the army guards with a group of prisoners he selected to perform that duty. He dressed the inmates in military uniforms and offered them classes in English language, art, guard duty, and craftsmanship. Experienced educators Misses Sarah Mather and Rebecca Perrit, who lived in St. Augustine, volunteered to conduct the classes as did Mather's friend Harriet Beecher Stowe. He allowed inmates to teach archery and sell artwork, bows and arrows, polished sea beans, and other trinkets to visitors. He also encouraged townspeople to hire his wards for jobs they could do. When fire struck buildings close to the fort in the middle of the night, Pratt marched a troop of Indians with buckets and blankets to help put it out. The residents were grateful as the town had no fire department.

Pratt's program soon became well-known across the country. Distinguished visitors, including Harriet Beecher Stowe and others, came from a variety of places. The U.S. commissioner of education and the president of Amherst College wanted to see firsthand what Pratt was doing for the Indians. The lieutenant's experience convinced him that putting them in "civilized environments" was the only way to totally assimilate Indians. He wrote, "[the Indian] is born a blank, like all the rest of us. Transfer the savage born infant to the surroundings of a civilization and he will grow to possess a civilized language and habit." By the end of the three-year sentences, he had erased any doubts he might have previously held about the conversion. He was completely convinced assimilation was the only way for Indians to survive in a modern society. Others considered Indians "a vanishing race" and thought it pointless to waste money and energy on them.

In his memoir, he wrote of an early example of assimilation that was working too well. "One of the prominent young ladies of St. Augustine was a special friend to the youngest Cheyenne." The girl kept the boy out after curfew and Pratt punished him. "A light stick of wood was given to him to carry on his shoulder [in lieu of a rifle] in front of the guard tent until midnight. I awakened at daylight and, looking out of the tent, saw the boy still carrying the stick of wood. Calling for the sergeant of the guard, who belonged to the same tribe, I asked why he had not relieved the young Indian. The sergeant of the guard replied that it was a very bad thing the boy had done and that my punishment was not severe enough, so he had kept him up all night."

When their confinement ended, Lt. Pratt convinced seventeen of his former prisoners to pursue further education at Hampton Institute (now Hampton University). The Hampton, Virginia school had been founded a decade earlier by Gen. Samuel Chapman Armstrong as a boarding school to educate recently freed slaves by training "the head, the hand, and the heart." Educating African-Americans and American Indians, although segregated from each other as well as the townspeople, was controversial to some as many thought Blacks and Indians were not educable. He differed from Armstrong, thinking full emersion into the majority culture was the key to Indians' long-term survival and left Hampton after a year. However, the experiment was successful enough that Hampton Institute continued its Indian division until 1923.

Richard Henry Pratt, son of a singing Methodist mother, summarized his philosophy as, "Kill the Indian, save the man." He viewed the reservations as ghettos in which Indians were denied the rights and opportunities enjoyed by citizens. Residents were afflicted by several pathologies prevalent on the reservations. Alcoholism, idleness, disease, violence, and polygamy were all too common. Many children were missing a parent, some two, and the tribes had few resources for orphans. One of the things that made Carlisle attractive to girls was that being hundreds or thousands of miles from home would make being married off to an old man as his second, third, or fourth wife difficult. To Pratt, killing the Indian meant stripping him of or keeping him from assimilating these pathologies. He viewed Indians being the same as other human beings and capable of accomplishing what any other race can. An important step was teaching the boys, and some girls, trades with which they could support themselves and not have to rely on meager government handouts for survival.

Pratt formulated a model similar to that being used at Hampton and successfully lobbied the government to set up a school just for Indians at an unused Army post adjacent to Carlisle, Pennsylvania. The former cavalry school had been abandoned in 1872 after local residents petitioned the War Department to stop Sunday dress parades. Fearful the townspeople would reject a school for Indians in their midst, Secretary of War George Washington McCrary directed Pratt to go to Carlisle and get a petition for the school. In Harrisburg while waiting for the Cumberland Valley RR train to Carlisle, Pratt told Gen. Chapman Biddle, then treasurer of the railroad, of his mission. Biddle told him to return to Washington saying, "I will send the Secretary a petition signed by every man and woman in Carlisle." Pratt did as Biddle suggested and received the petition a few days later. The railroad executive probably told merchants about the commerce the school would bring and townspeople the jobs it would create.

Congress approved the use of Carlisle Barracks by the Department of the Interior and detailed Pratt for Indian education duty. The War Department issued the order and Lt. and Mrs. Pratt were on their way to Carlisle. No sooner were Mrs. Pratt and the children settled in and a builder arranged to make necessary repairs and improvements, Pratt traveled to the Dakotas to recruit students for the school. His orders called for him to get thirty-six pupils each from the Rosebud and Pine Ridge Reservations and to get enough more from the Indian Territory (Oklahoma) tribes to bring the total to 120 students. Miss Sarah Mather, then considered aged at sixty-three, urged him to let her accompany him on the trip to help with the girls.

Pratt and Mather took a train to Yankton where they caught a boat that took them up the Missouri River to a landing one hundred miles from Rosebud Reservation. The new agent there sent a two-seated spring wagon to meet them. The Indian driver brought four blankets for his use and none for his passengers. Pratt recalled:

> "I determined to make the trip in two days, so sat with the driver, used the 'black snake' whip, and kept the mules at the necessary speed. When halfway, we stopped for the night. We made Miss Mather an army bed in the bottom of the wagon, taking out the seats, using a cushion for a pillow, and giving her two of the blankets which, by folding, we made into a camp bag bed with two thicknesses above and two below. The Indian and I slept under the wagon using the other two blankets, one to sleep on and one over us. We all slept in our clothing. It was a frosty night and we suffered from the cold. There being no other way, we had to hitch the mules to the wagon. Wolves came near and howled, and once I got up with my revolver to drive them away, but they were too far off to shoot. Sleep was practically impossible for me. The cold led us to start long before daylight. During the afternoon Miss Mather became wretchedly seasick and we had to stop several times. We reached the agency before dark and the very capable agency physician soon restored her equilibrium."

Initially, the agency employees and chiefs objected to sending the children so far away but, after passing a ceremonial pipe around a circle of forty chiefs and elders, Pratt made his pitch. Spotted Tail, the principal chief, spoke against their children learning the white man's wicked ways. Pratt countered with the argument that, had the Indians been able to read and write, they wouldn't have been cheated when signing treaties. After talking among themselves, the chiefs agreed to send their children to Carlisle.

The next morning, Pratt set out for the Pine Ridge Agency. This time he asked for a light wagon and two ponies. The driver, who spoke no English, navigated the hundred-mile trip more quickly than had the previous driver. When darkness fell, they followed the stars and arrived well before midnight. Red Cloud was old and had no young children. However, he agreed to send a grandson. Pratt was able to enroll only sixteen, mostly boys, from Pine Ridge.

When he returned to Rosebud, ninety children waited to enroll. The agency physician and his wife gave the children careful physical examinations before Pratt would accept them. He only took fifty-six of them because he was only authorized a total of seventy-two from the Dakotas. He later decided to add ten more in accordance with the Indian Bureau's idea that having the children in white men's hands would be a deterrent to war. When he called roll on the boat at the landing, two additional boys from Pine Ridge were found to be stowaways. When Pratt attempted to put them ashore, the Pine Ridge agent convince him to let them stay. He now had eighty-four students enrolled, twelve more than were authorized.

Pratt noticed that nearly all of the boys were smoking cigarettes as they steamed down the river. He then bought all that were for sale and handed them out to the boys with this admonition: "Between here and Carlisle, as we will be traveling on the boat and as on the [train]cars the boys will be in a separate car from the girls, we can all have a goodbye smoke all the way to Carlisle, but when we reach Carlisle we will all quit." He knew he would have to break his twelve-year habit when he reached the school and broke it cold turkey.

Around midnight on October 6, 1879, hundreds of people from the town greeted Pratt and the first contingent of students to arrive at the school. The townspeople escorted the tired travelers on the walk from Carlisle Junction to the barracks. The first group of students were largely sons of Lakota chiefs (boys had little economic value when confined to reservations because they could no longer hunt buffalo or make war, but families could still receive a bride price for girls, often in ponies). America's second-oldest military facility—the one that housed Hessian troops captured at Trenton by Gen. George Washington after crossing the Delaware—now housed the children of warriors who only three years earlier had defeated Custer at the Battle of the Little Bighorn.

Shortly after the students from Indian Territory arrived, three Quaker ladies came for a visit: Miss Susan Longstreth and her sister Mary Anna, then retired after operating a famous school for young ladies in Philadelphia for 50 years, and a Miss Brown, one of their former students. After a tour of the school, Miss Longstreth asked, "Captain, thee is undertaking a great work here. Thee will need many things. Thee must remember if thee would receive thee must ask. Will thee take thy pencil and put down some of the things thee needs very much just now and the cost?"

Pratt listed tools needed for the various shops for the trades the students would study. The women took his list and huddled. Pratt heard them say, "I will take this" and "I will take that." Miss Longstreth handed him back the list, saying, "Buy all and send us the amount of each bill, and we will send checks to pay." He felt the same rush of blood to his brain and heart forty-two years afterward as he did when it happened. The Quaker ladies from Philadelphia continued to support Pratt and Carlisle until their deaths.

Carlisle Indian Industrial School students divided their days between academic studies and vocational training. They dressed in military uniforms and lived regimented lives. Free-time activities included music, athletics, and literary or debating societies. Although Carlisle Indian Industrial School was essentially a trade school coupled to elementary and high school academics, Pratt envisioned some of his students advancing to college and professional schools.

Rather than returning to their reservations during school breaks, Pratt wanted his students kept away from tribal influences as long as possible, ideally their entire enrollment periods. During their "outing" periods working off-campus at farms and businesses to further immerse them in the dominant culture, students received practical experience and made some money of which they were forced to save a significant portion. Pratt kept his charges away from their families and tribes three, four, or five years at a time, depending on when they enrolled. In 1883, explaining his philosophy, he wrote, "In Indian civilization I am a Baptist, because I believe in immersing the Indians in our civilization and when we get them under holding them there until they are thoroughly soaked." The government saved money by not having to house and feed the children when they were away.

As the school's superintendent, Pratt constantly battled Congress for funding and did not fare well. He was not shy about publicly criticizing the government's stinginess and other shortcomings, particularly those in the Bureau of Indian Affairs. The outing period wasn't enough to keep costs within budget; other funding sources were needed. Donations from individuals helped immensely.

Extracurricular activities, particularly the literary and debating societies, helped prepare higher-level students for further academic work as well as to think more critically and to communicate more clearly, skills that would serve future leaders well. Although Pratt desired that his former students assimilate into the dominant culture, many returned to their tribes and used the skills learned at Carlisle to become effective tribal leaders. Others returned to their former ways.

Soon, the girls and boys each had two societies from which to select: the Susan Longstreth Literary Society, the Mercer Literary Society, the Standard Debating Society, and the Invincible Debating Society, respectively. These societies were much more than what their names implied as some of them formed bands, played sports, held dances, and put on plays. They also had their own colors and elected officers as did the freshman, sophomore, junior and senior classes. Carlisle's classes (freshman et al) did not correspond to public high school classes of the same names. Besides the usual officers, these groups elected a Critic, whose function may not be obvious to modern readers. The author found a definition in the *1918 Quittapahilla,* Lebanon Valley College's yearbook: "Over each meeting presides the Critic and he, by mode of criticism, points out the strength and weakness of the respective numbers with special reference to errors in style, English grammar, elocution, logic, literary structure and the speakers' manner on the floor." While some of the details may vary between schools and organizations, the description will hold in the main.

The boys loved playing games and sports. In the early years of the school, they played the games they had played on the reservations. Over time, they adopted the sports schoolboys across the country enjoyed. At Carlisle, each shop had its own athletic teams that competed in intramurals with the others on campus. The annual shop football championship was a major event. In 1890, some of the boys played off-campus against the Dickinson College team. Having had little direct experience with football and seeing occasional victims of the game's violence, Captain Pratt was not disposed to encourage its playing. When Stacy Matlock suffered a compound fracture of his lower leg in the Dickinson game, Pratt carried him from the carriage to the operating table. He helped hold the boy while the doctor set the break. Revulsed by what he saw, Pratt decreed, "This ends outside football for us."

Competitive Football's Birth at Carlisle

One fall afternoon in 1893, Richard Henry Pratt, superintendent of Carlisle Indian School, worked at his desk in the headquarters building on Carlisle Barracks, the army's second-oldest installation behind West Point. Established in 1787 by British Col. John Stanwix and nestled in picturesque Cumberland Valley, Carlisle Barracks served as a supply post during the French and Indian War. Prior to the Civil War, it housed a cavalry school. The headquarters building, like almost everything on the base, was relatively new, built after 1863. The only pre-Civil War structure remaining was the limestone powder magazine built by Hessian soldiers taken prisoner by Washington at Trenton. Everything else was burned in July 1863 by J. E. B. Stuart's Confederate troops while the Battle of Gettysburg raged in the next county south.

A knock on the door interrupted this Civil War hero and leader of Buffalo Soldiers. Dressed in his blue cavalry officer's uniform, although working at detached assignments since 1878, Richard Henry Pratt, the epitome of *loco parentis,* considered the students, who ranged in age from four to twenty-four, as his children and believed it was his responsibility to look after them. He often referred to himself as their "school father." Capt. Pratt even gave the brides away in his full dress uniform when they married. Wanting to give students educational experiences similar to what whites got, a range of clubs and activities such as the YMCA and debating societies were organized. He succeeded in getting a Quaker lady to donate the money to start a school band. Pratt allowed the boys to form intramural football teams representing the various shops, clubs, and even the band. He could control what happened on campus but not elsewhere. In 1890, Stacy Matlock's leg was badly broken in a sandlot game with the Dickinson College team. Helping the school physician set the compound fracture revulsed Pratt so terribly he banned off-campus football.

The superintendent told the unseen visitor to enter and his door opened, revealing forty of the school's finest athletes dressed in their best military uniforms with something on their minds. At over six feet tall and with a face that reflected his near-death experience with smallpox as a child, Capt. Pratt presented a commanding appearance. In spite of this, students felt comfortable approaching him with their problems and requests. He invited the boys into his office where they stood around his desk, their black eyes intensely focused on him. The school's champion orator, possibly Benjamin Caswell, stepped forward and presented himself as a descendent of Chief Logan.

He began, "I appeal to any white man to say that ever he entered Logan's cabin hungry and he gave him no meat, came cold and naked and he clothed him not." The boy then presented the case for playing football against other schools eloquently.

Pratt recalled: "...[T]he genius of his argument almost compelled me to relax the judicial mien and release any pent-up laughter. When he had finished, I waited a little and then said: 'Boys, I begin to realize that I must surrender and give you the opportunities you so earnestly desire. I will let you take up outside football again, under two conditions.'

"'First, that you will never, under any circumstances, slug. That you will play fair straight through. And if the other fellows slug you will in no case return it. Can't you see that if you slug, people who are looking on will say, 'There, that's the Indian of it. Just see them. They are savages and you can't get it out of them.' Our white fellows may do a lot of slugging and it causes little or no remark, but you have to make a record for your race. If the other fellows slug and you do not return it, very soon you will be the most famous football team in the country. If you can set an example of that kind for the white race, you will do a work in the highest interests of your people.'"

The boys responded in unison, "All right, Captain. We agree to that."

"My other condition is this. That, in the course of two, three, or four years, you will develop your strength and ability to such a degree that you will whip the biggest football team in the country. Well, what do you say to that?"

The boys stood silent before their spokesman said, "Well, Captain, we will try."

Pratt responded, "I don't want you to promise to try. I want you to say that you will do it. The man who only thinks of trying to do a thing admits to himself that he may fail, while the sure winner is the man who will not admit to failure. You must get your determination up to that point."

Looking serious, they thought for a while before answering, "Yes sir, we will agree to that."

Pleased, Pratt said, "Very well, now I know that you cannot win unless you have as good or better instruction than your opponents, and I will write to Walter Camp, the great football authority, and ask him to name me the best coach in the United States and, if possible to get him, he will be your instructor."

Ecstatic, the boys left.

Pratt followed through and wrote Camp. "The father of American football" responded promptly with the name Glenn Scobey "Pop" Warner, who was then engaged as the head coach of his alma mater, Cornell. The ingenious Warner sounded like the right man but he wasn't available. So, Pratt delegated the job to his second-in-command, Disciplinarian William G. Thompson. He had no known experience coaching football; he was an administrator and taught business courses. But it was much too late in the season for anything resembling a full schedule. So, Thompson hurriedly arranged three games, two of which were with area high school teams.

With only 250 to 300 boys of age to play on the school's football team, Carlisle was at a disadvantage to the colleges and universities the Indians would be playing. Those schools generally had largely male student bodies numbering in the thousands and footballers who had played on their high school or prep school teams. Many of the Carlislian eleven hadn't even seen a football before coming to the Indian School.

One advantage Carlisle had before 1914 was, because many of its players were older than white children when they began their education, they were older and more physically and emotionally mature than their opponents. Another reason for Carlisle having older players was that it wasn't unusual for its students to re-enroll for an additional period to continue their education.

Although Carlisle was a vocational school in which students spent half the day in academic classes, the other half learning a trade, some graduated from high school and a few graduated from college. Dickinson School of Law was where most Carlisle players who earned degrees got theirs. They chose the Law School because they could start earning money immediately after graduating. A couple went to dental school later.

Over half of Carlisle's players had lost at least one parent and several had lost both. The Indian School gave them places to live and, in some cases, opportunities to earn money to pay tuition at an off-campus institution. To some extent, Carlisle served as an orphanage because the reservations had limited finances and little to support orphaned children.

Team captains in those days were much more important than today, where the title is mostly ceremonial. In the early years of American football, the captain was responsible for running the team during games. Coaching from the sidelines and sending in plays was barred. Players were supposed to be smart enough to call their own plays.

Cheating on this rule was common as players, coaches, and water boys concocted ways of communicating from the sidelines to the players on the field. Carlisle was no different from the colleges in this regard.

The players elected a member as their leader and followed his directions. The captain could play any position as leadership qualities were the most important factor. Benjamin Caswell, class of '92, then attending the Dickinson College prep school, was selected as Carlisle's first captain, probably because of having experience playing college football on the Dickinson team the year before.

Football was a violent games in those days. Players were frequently maimed and some died each year. Opposing teams lined-up against each other literally toe-to-toe, waiting for the ball to be snapped. Mass plays, in which punching, kicking, and biting were largely hidden from officials, dominated the game. Brutal wedge plays, in which players would lock arms or hang onto each other to produce an impregnable wall in front of the ballcarrier, had been introduced the year before, and experts expected them to be used more widely this year. Had Pratt known that, he might have made a different decision. Regardless, Carlisle was soon using the V, as some reporters called it, in their offense.

On Saturday, November 11, 1893, the Carlisle Indians took the field as an official NCAA (retroactively) team when they faced off against Harrisburg High School. *The Philadelphia Inquirer* listed the game as a scoreless tie between Carlisle Training School and Harrisburg High. *The Harrisburg Patriot* gave the Indians the win at 10-0, listing the Harrisburg players' names but not Carlisle's.

Two days later, the Indians played Dickinson College on its own field. The college's newspaper, *The Dickinsonian,* reported, "Quite a large crowd passed through the gates for the main purpose of seeing the Indians play football [sic], and all went away with the knowledge that Indians can play this exceedingly popular game as well as base-ball [sic]." Fumbles were the Indians' downfall but they fought to the end of the forty-minute skirmish. Benjamin Caswell had to leave the game due to a serious leg injury. "The Indians played a plucky, obstinate game from start to finish." The college boys beat their neighbors but considered this to be a practice game and didn't compile detailed statistics.

The Dickinsonian gave the score as 16-0, but the text of the article suggested that the published result omitted a touchdown the Indians scored: "The Indian perseverance and determination then showed itself. They bucked our centre [sic] until they carried the ball over the line but failed to kick goal."[1]

---

[1] At that time, extra points after touchdowns required a player from the team scoring the touchdown to punt the ball from the spot behind the goal line where

Making a touchdown was worth four points, six if the kick after was successful. *The Patriot* reported the score as 16-4, as the game coverage supported.

On Thanksgiving Day, November 30, Carlisle played another Indian school, Educational Home (later Lincoln Institute) of Philadelphia, on the Dickinson College field. (The future Red Devils were away at Harrisburg's Island Park playing Bucknell that day.) Carlisle easily shut out the visiting Indians, scoring six touchdowns and kicking five field goals for a total of thirty-four points in the forty-five-minute first half. They pushed across two more touchdowns and made both kicks after touchdown in the twenty-minute second half for a total of seven out of eight attempts for the game. These scores totaled forty-six points for Carlisle, instead of the fifty *The Sentinel* headline blared. Perhaps they made another touchdown or two safeties the reporter missed. The fifty probably came from the scoreboard, so we'll use that until more information is uncovered.

Caswell, Jonas Metoxen, Bemus Pierce, and Laban Locojim starred for Carlisle. Fairbanks and Peake did well for Philadelphia, but Carlisle's line was too heavy for them.

Position	Player
Right End	Laban Locojim (Apache)
Right Tackle	Joseph Irwin (Gros Ventre)
Right Guard	Bemus Pierce (Seneca)
Center	Benjamin Doxtator (Oneida)
Left Guard	Martin Wheelock (Oneida)
Left Tackle	Charles Buck (Piegan)
Left End	Anthony Austin (Piegan)
Quarterback	Harvey Warner (Omaha)
Right Halfback	Benjamin Caswell (Chippewa)
Left Halfback	Frank Cayou (Omaha)
Fullback	Jonas Metoxen (Oneida)

A number of young men wanting to see the game without paying the fifteen-cent ticket price tried to scale the fence surrounding the Dickinson College athletic field. One who succeeded was captured by an Indian guard and ordered to get out. The man refused and started a fight that drew in several others. When policemen stopped the melee, a crowd outside hurled

---

the ball was touched down to a teammate a prescribed distance away. The person receiving the punt would call a fair catch. A dropkick or placekick would be attempted from that spot.

stones onto the field. Officer Jackson approached the fence to get the people to stop. Instead, someone threw a large stone that hit him between the eyes. The unfortunate policeman was knocked unconscious. The attending physician feared that Jackson's skull was fractured. Luckily, it wasn't. After that, Pratt attended as many games as practical to prevent future problems.

Intercollegiate football at Carlisle was born, although Carlisle Indian Industrial School was never a college, but the vast majority of the opponents they would soon be scheduling most certainly were.

Why Would Indians Be Good at Football?

Some pundits cited reasons why they thought Indian athletes should outperform their white counterparts. R. Meade Bache, a longtime scientist with the U. S. Coast and Geodetic Survey, wrote articles about the physical force imparted by boxers' muscles and got them published in scientific journals. His 1895 paper on reaction times by race attracted the attention of University of Pennsylvania Professor of Psychology Lightner Witmer, who applied an electrical shock to the wrists of a dozen young men of three races and timed how soon they responded using a telegrapher's key. In Witmer's experiment, whites had the slowest reaction times and Indians the quickest. Blacks' times were in between. Bache explained away the Indians' faster reaction times than Blacks as the result of the Blacks having had intermarried more with whites than had Indians.

The Philadelphia Inquirer reporter covering Penn's football game with Carlisle that fall shifted the differences from genetics to culture: "[The Indians] saw more quickly, heard and responded to all sensations more quickly. Mr. Bache's theory is that the higher the civilization the greater the loss in quickness of automatic movements." After the game, long-time Penn football Coach George Woodruff reportedly said "[H]e would rather train the Indian boys than his own team and that they composed the ideal team for which he has been long looking would seem to sustain the purely scientific experiments." It seems logical that young men who have spent their lives living in nature and observing animals while hunting would develop quicker reflexes than those who lived in towns and cities.

Later, Pop Warner made observations of his own players. He noticed both physical and cultural differences. He claimed that Indians' lower legs dropped straight down from the knee where whites' lower legs curved slightly outward. Carlisle publicist Hugh R. Miller maintained that most Indians' feet were flat, parallel to each other, and pointed straight ahead where whites' pointed outward. (The author, a subject group of one white person, noticed the reasons he was a poor kicker. His lower legs curve slightly and that his toes point outward.) Warner thought straight lower legs gave Indian kickers an advantage. And Indians could get kicks off slightly quicker because their feet were already pointed straight ahead where white kickers had to turn their foot to put it in the proper position.[2] To the author's knowledge, this claim hasn't been researched. His experience coaching Indian players led Warner to observe how they learned:

> "While at Carlisle, I had developed a theory that the Indians boys had been trained by their forefathers to be keen observers. Often when the Indian boys were exposed to a new sport or game, they would usually refuse to participate. Instead they would stand and watch the older, more experienced Indian boys, who were participating in the new sport or game, demonstrate how it was to be played.
>
> "Then after having studied the play or actions of the elders, they would attempt to mimic those same actions, or motions, and would usually be almost as accomplished as those who they had just observed."

Carlisle Indian School, created and operated by cavalry officer Richard Henry Pratt and located on the Army's second-oldest post, was a construct of the Federal Government. Dependent on government funding, it was an endangered species on the edge of extinction its entire existence. As early as 1898, success on the football field aided its survival against political opposition. This was not the last time football came to the school's assistance.

During his twenty-five-year tenure as superintendent, the school and everything it did reflected Pratt's views and opinions. Following superintendents were either cavalry officers or government employees, and the football team, although "owned" by the athletic association, was not exempt from government influence and policies, which changed over time.

---

[2] A tracker in an old Hollywood western opined that a white man had joined a group he was trailing because his toes pointed outward where the others pointed straight ahead. Warner's belief may not have been as uncommon as it seemed.

This book is primarily about the players themselves, the most colorful to ever don football togs, and not just because some were inducted into the Hall of Fame. Their lives and personalities were often much more interesting than the scions of the wealthy they played against.

Looking back in later years after winning national championships and the Rose Bowl while leading other teams, Warner fondly remembered the Indians:

> "Great teams, those Carlisle elevens that I coached, and what was even finer, sportsmen all. There wasn't an Indian of the lot who didn't love to win and hate to lose, but to a man they were modest in victory and resolute in defeat. They never gloated, they never whined, and no matter how bitter the contest, they played cheerfully, squarely, and cleanly."

Superintendent Pratt with young student.

Chauncey Edward Archiquette arrived in Carlisle on September 21, 1890 at 12 years of age to begin a five-year term of enrollment. That week's edition of *The Indian Helper* announced his arrival:

> "Peter Powlas brought with him from Oneida Wisconsin: Lucinda Kick, Melinda Metoxen, Lydia Powlas, Melissa Green, Ophelia King, Alice Powlas, Moses King, Isaac Metoxen, Martin Wheelock, Taylor Smith, Whitney Powlas, John Powlas, Chauncey Archiquette, Brigman Cornelius, and Isaac John."

By virtue of having neighbors and siblings at the school, he most certainly would not have been lonely. He went out on two outings

Name:	Chauncey Edward Archiquette	Nickname:	
DOB:	11/17/1877	Height:	5'7"
Weight:	158 lbs.	Age:	21
Parents:	John Archiquette Elizabeth Smith Archiquette	Home:	Green Bay, WI
Early Schooling:	Unknown		
Later Schooling:	Haskell Institute		

From left to right: Chauncey Archiquette, Capt. Charles Roy & Charles "Wahoo" Guyon on 1906 CIIS baseball team

during his first enrollment, one of which was quite lengthy as it lasted almost 17 months. He received little other mention during that time, but that wouldn't last forever.

After his term was up in June 1895, he returned home just for the summer. In the fall, he enrolled for another five-year term. Now that Chauncey was a large boy, he became more active in extra-curricular activities and thus received more mention in school publications. In April 1896, he became an officer of the Invincible Debating Society by serving as sergeant-at-arms. That month he also became the starting left fielder for the varsity baseball team. In the fall, he played football but didn't get into any varsity games. Prior to 1896, he probably played on his shop team and moved up to the Junior Varsity or the Second Team. However, almost no records exist for those teams and their games. The May 28, 1897 issue of *The Indian Helper* included a little riddle: "Why should Archiquette be called 'Flour and Eggs?' Because he makes a good batter." That riddle immediately followed the write-up of a game with Gettysburg College the Indians won 27-1. Unfortunately, no box score was included. However, the riddle implies Chauncey had a good day.

Sports weren't allowed to take up all his time. Archiquette spent half his days in the harness-making shop, learning that trade. The other half of his school day was spent in academic classes. The fall of 1897 was his break-out year in football. He played right end on a team that went 6-4, losing to Princeton, Yale, Penn and Brown, scoring on all but Princeton.

The next summer he played baseball again. In August, 1898, the all-seeing "Man-on-the-band-stand" noticed his baseball playing and wrote, "Ah, Chauncey Archiquette is making a home-run, and another, see? He is the star catcher in the field, too."

That fall, Chauncey was a member of the Senior Class and played right end again on the football team. The 1898 team, the last one before Pop Warner was first hired, went 5-4, losing to three of the Big Four, again, and Cornell, scoring in all of their losses. He graduated in February and returned home in March. However, he didn't stay there long.

Chauncey then enrolled at Haskell Institute, in the commercial program most likely, and also played sports. He also played baseball in the summer, probably for Haskell. At summer's end, it was back to school for Chauncey. He found himself in a familiar position that fall— at the right end of the Haskell Indians' line. His first mention for his football playing at that school was a dubious one: he was ejected from the first game against Fielding Yost's team, cross-town rival Kansas, for slugging. Apparently, these games were grudge matches because the Indians walked off the field early in the second half of the rematch in mid-season. Although Haskell was shut out in both games, by scores of 12-0 and 18-0, respectively, they held the 10-0-0 Jayhawkers to their lowest scores of the season. Haskell, ended up at 4-5-0 but Archiquette apparently impressed his new teammates because they elected him captain of the 1900 team. They made a good choice.

Haskell started their season with a 28-0 defeat of Kansas State Normal College of Emporia, Kansas. Their next opponent, the University of Missouri, was waiting for them. *The Lincoln Evening News*, in a demonstration of objectivity, observed,

> "The Missourians had been expecting so much from their pets, too, that the result was heart rending. They started the season with a hurrah and a bluff that they could lick all opponents. Three coaches were hired, a mass meeting of students was called, subscriptions for the support of the team poured in, and all was roseate and promising. But now a dark cloud overhangs the future...Tigers repeatedly dropped the ball, especially in trying to catch punts, and one of those bobbles by Hogan gave Haskell a touchdown. Captain Archiquette got the ball, and with a clean field, sprinted across the goal line."

Haskell shut out Mizzou 11-0. They would go on to a 9-1-0 season, losing their last game to Washburn College, a team they had beaten the first time they met earlier in the season. Only four of their opponents scored on them—three actually because Washburn scored in both of its games. Chauncey played basketball in the winter and baseball in spring and summer before football season rolled around again.

Haskell's 1901 season started off with three easy victories over weak opponents. On November 4, they met the University of Minnesota in what was described beforehand as the biggest game Haskell had ever played. The *Lincoln Evening News* reported,

> "The Haskell men are confident of winning from Minnesota. They recognize the fact that the Gophers play a great deal stronger game than any other team Haskell has ever met, but they are prepared to put up the game of their lives."

Sportswriters found that several former Carlisle players would be in the game. They couldn't have known that some future ones were there as well. Captain Archiquette—he was elected again—played opposite Ed Rogers, last year's Carlisle captain but that year a Gopher. Thaddeus Red Water, Haskell's left guard, had also played for Carlisle the year before. Left tackle William Baine was at Carlisle the previous year and Charlie Guyon, who was not at Haskell that year, met up with the team in Minneapolis to play left end. Newspapers hyped the impending battle between Archiquette and Rogers, "The struggle of these two men alone will be well worth seeing, as the Haskell captain is said to be one of the fastest Indian players in football this fall." The Indians' hopes were dashed in a 28-0 loss. Five days later, they rebounded and beat John Outland's Kansas team 18-5. Next they beat Missouri and two smaller schools. Their 7-2-0 season ended with an 18-10 Thanksgiving Day loss to Nebraska. In his two years as captain, Archiquette was 16-3-0. Not bad at all.

A summer of playing first base for the Haskell team followed a winter of basketball for Archiquette. And some winter it was! Haskell claimed the national championship after defeating the M. W. A. team of Independence, Missouri, previous claimants to the title. The win was by way of forfeit when, early in the second half, with Haskell leading 17-15, the Missourians left the court, complaining of unfair treatment even though two of the three officials were from Missouri. Haskell's victims included teams from the Universities of Nebraska and Kansas.

Chauncey was no longer a student after graduating from the Commercial Department in the spring. He was then hired as Assistant Disciplinarian at the school. In what seemed to be an annual coaching change, John Outland took the reins as head coach of the 1902 squad. Fallis was team captain and Chauncey played right halfback. In addition to the new coach, the team was also greeted by another upgraded schedule. Even with that, the Indians finished 9-4-1 with losses to Illinois, Nebraska, Bethany College and Kansas State. Their wins included victories over Kansas State, Missouri, Texas, and Kansas. The Kansas game, in which he scored two touchdowns, was a personal highlight for Chauncey.

In January 1903, *The Lincoln Evening News* contradicted *The Indian Leader* by stating that the Haskell Indians had won the basketball championship of the West the previous year (instead of the National Championship), but expected them to repeat after a 35-18 defeat of Dr. James Naismith's Kansas University team. They didn't repeat but had a good season that included a tour east of the Mississippi. That summer, Chauncey played first base and batted clean-up for the Nebraska Indians. He was also team captain. A new man seldom gets those honors, so he may have played for them in earlier seasons. The Nebraska Indians were a barnstorming team that traveled across the Midwest and even crossed the Mississippi on occasion. They had a phenomenally high won-loss record, but often competed against teams whose players had day jobs. The Indians' players devoted their summers to baseball and became very good at it.

The 1903 football season started promisingly with a 45-0 thrashing of Colorado College and a 6-0 win over Texas. Next up on the schedule were the always-tough Nebraskans whose Coach "Bummy" Booth threatened to take Haskell off his schedule because of their lax eligibility rules. Martin Wheelock's recent transfer to Haskell from Carlisle prompted his outburst. The game start was delayed over an hour in a dispute over using an old Kansas man named Tucker as an official. Eventually Booth allowed Tucker to be used. The Indians lost 16-0 but bounced back with wins over Kansas and Missouri. Next up was a big game with Amos Alonzo Stagg's Chicago team. The Indians played the Maroons to a standstill but scored fewer points. They then ran off three straight wins before losing badly to Kansas State to end the season. 7-3-

0 under a first-year coach wasn't bad. In fact, their play prompted promotion of a post-season game between Carlisle and Haskell. But that was not to be—not yet, anyway. Charles Guyon, who had returned to Haskell, was elected captain for 1904.

In the middle of another fine basketball campaign, reports stating that Chauncey might be turning pro hit the papers:

> "Archiquette, the Indian who played on Haskell football team for the past three years as quarter and end, is to be given a try-out with the Kansas City Blues at center field. He is a fast and heady player, and those who have seen him play will agree that he stands a good chance. He is an artist at unhooking the long ones, and a hard hitter. He uses a bat about four inches longer than the limit and when he lands it is all over. He has played with the Haskell Indian baseball team around the state for several years."

A wire service article elaborated a bit:

> "This new Blue is a graduate of Haskell and is one of the best-known athletes of the West. He has made his name famous as a football player, and has added further laurels to his athletic prowess as being equally good at baseball. Those who have seen him play say that he is lightning on his feet and is a sure fielder. He will prove a drawing card, if he does not find the company too fast."

He must not have made the team or his over-sized bat was not allowed because, in the fall, he was back out on the gridiron in a Haskell uniform. The 1904 season started auspiciously with ecumenical thrashings of the Quakers of Friends University and the Baptists of Ottawa University. The Indians' first real test was their cross-town rival, Kansas University, whom they beat convincingly, 23-6. They dispatched Missouri by a wider margin, 39-0. They found the lot at Austin much tougher and were stalemated until Pete Hauser kicked a 45-yard field goal, the game's only score, one that barely cleared the crossbar. After Ottawa canceled a rematch, all that stood between them and the

Missouri Valley Championship was their nemesis, Nebraska. Cornhusker coach Bummy Booth didn't show the Indians much respect:

> "This is the fourth year we have played the Indians, and every year we have counted on a hard game and found a comparatively easy one. We don't like this game, but we have to play it, and that means that we are going to play it hard and give these people all they want this year. The players, with the exception of Captain Benedict, are in good shape, and they ought to be able to play as well Saturday as any time this year. Benedict will be able to get in the game, I think, and we can put up as good a front against them as we did against Minnesota. I know these Indians, nearly every one of them, and I know just what they can do. So when I say that we are going to win from them by at least fifty points, I ought to have a little idea of what I am talking about The Nebraskans are getting into the game well in the past few days and they are going to play against those Indians as hard or harder, if possible than they did against the Gophers."

On November 10, under the headline, "Booth Predicts Score of Sixty to Nothing," *The Lincoln Evening News* doubted the game would be played:

> "There is still a possibility, even at this late date, that the Haskell-Nebraska game, scheduled for Kansas City Saturday will be called off. Manager Davis has received a telegram from Coach John Outland of Washburn who had been selected for referee, declaring that under no consideration will he officiate at the game. This announcement took the local authorities off their feet, as they had thought the official question settled when Hoagland and Outland had been decided on a week ago. The question of choosing a referee will now take up the time until the game, and it may prove an insurmountable obstruction. The Haskell management announced some time ago that it would consider no Nebraska man as an official, and Manager Davis said this morning that he was stumped as to a man to suggest.

Haskell evidently thinks they will get the worst of the deal, and they seem to be looking for a man who will help them out in doubtful situations."

The article brought up the fact that officials were not the only controversy:

"Coach Herrnstein, of the Haskell Indian team, insists that [John] Warren, the big Indian guard, who will probably go into the game against Nebraska, is not in any sense a 'ringer,' and was not brought to Haskell especially for this game. 'The idea that Warren is there solely to play football is a mistake,' he said, speaking about the matter while in Kansas City Sunday night. 'He is taking regular work there, and is right in line for a good position in the school. He is an expert harness-maker, and if the superintendent of the harness shops resigns, as is now his intention, Warren will probably succeed him in that position. He had been planning for some time to come to Haskell, and hastened his coming a little in order to join our party as we were coming back from the Texas trip.'

"I have been opposed all along to the mystery which has been thrown around his identity and did not give him the name of 'Big Chief' or 'Big Brave.' That was started by some Lawrence correspondents, and some of the people at the school thought that it might increase the interest in the team to let it go on that way."

In spite of everything, Nebraska kicked off on time at 2:35 p.m. with John Outland as referee, Ralph Hoagland as umpire, and Lt. Cosad as head linesman. Pete Hauser kicked a field goal to complete Haskell's first possession. Nebraska was stopped on downs and was forced to punt. After a 15-yard return, a 15-yard off-side penalty against Nebraska, and a 40-yard run by Moore to the 5-yard line, Porter carried the ball over for a touchdown. By making the kick after touchdown, the score was Haskell 10, Nebraska 0. After Nebraska got the ball, they were unable to make a first down and punted the ball back. Pete Hauser immediately kicked a 40-yard field goal. Haskell 14, Nebraska

0. Haskell got the ball back after a fumble on Nebraska's 35. Archiquette carried the ball around his left end for a 15-yard gain but fumbled it away. The half ended with no further scoring. The only scoring in the second half was Bender's 23-yard field goal and a safety. That made the final score Haskell 14, Nebraska 6.

In the middle of the following week, Coach Herrnstein observed:

> "Elation over winning from Nebraska has not yet died down at Haskell institute. Emil Houser is the only man in bad shape. His face was trampled on and is badly lacerated. Fallis, Dubois, and Oliver are limping, but they will be all right in a few days. Archiquette, the star halfback, does not remember a play made in the second half. He does not know that he fumbled two punts and he asked the score three or four times while changing clothes before he could remember it. He stopped calling signals early in the second half. He could think of no-plays but those numbered five and he threw the team into confusion by continually calling thirty-five, forty-five and fifty-five plays that had no place in that part of the game. Fallis, and afterward, Moore, called the signals during the last of the game. When Emil Hauser went back to punt just before Nebraska made her-safety, it was Fallis' place to kick instead of Hauser's. Hauser had one eye shut and misjudged the distance as he stepped back. Standing so close to the center the ball naturally reached him high and hard."

About this time, the administration announced that Haskell would play a game against Carlisle at the St. Louis World's Fair the Saturday after Thanksgiving to coincide with President Roosevelt's visit. Haskell was scheduled to play Washington University of St. Louis at the Fair on Thanksgiving Day. The Indians annihilated the Crepe and Myrtle 42-0 or 47-0 (accounts vary), hardly breaking a sweat. Meanwhile, the Carlisle Second Team smashed the Ohio State eleven 23-0. Neither Indian team risked its best players in these warmup games. The main event came two days later. Although President Theodore Roosevelt didn't attend the game, the stadium was packed. Haskell moved the ball well early in a drive that was capped by a Pete Hauser field goal. That was all they would get. Carlisle prevailed 38-4. However, Haskell accomplished something Carlisle never did; they went undefeated through the regular season. Their sole loss this year was in the post-season. Carlisle's losses in the one-loss seasons were regular season games. Soon, Chauncey would be back at Carlisle and would be followed by some of his teammates. But there's more to the story as Jim Thorpe's biographer, Robert W. Wheeler, learned when he interviewed Thorpe's Haskell classmate and friend, George Washington.

If not the biggest, Chauncey Archiquette was one of the biggest men on campus. So big that younger boys tried to emulate him. One of them was a scrawny little boy named Jim Thorpe. After practice was over, the lad would run back and forth across the field in his best imitation of his idol. One day Chauncey noticed what the lad was up to and had a chat with him. Seeing that Jim was serious about wanting to play football, he put his Carlisle training to use and made the boy a football out of leather and stuffed it with rags. Now that he had a ball to play with, Jim organized games with other boys and improved so much that he started to compete with older boys in some athletic contests.

Chauncey returned to Carlisle in September 1905, after another summer of baseball, most likely. This time he wasn't a student but was putting what he learned in the Commercial Course at Haskell to work in his position as assistant clerk. The 1905 edition of the Carlisle Indians was a good one and portended the future greatness. Haskellites Charles Guyon, who was then going by the name of Wahoo, Alfred Dubois, and Scott Porter (Little Boy) also transferred to Carlisle that year. Others would follow in future years. George Woodruff, Hall of Fame Coach most closely associated with Penn was advisory coach that year. He was assisted by Ralph Kinney, a first team All-American fresh from Yale, as well as two former Carlisle stars, Bemus Pierce and Frank Hudson.

Chauncey continued to play right halfback as he had in his later years at Haskell. The first three games were won by an average margin of 51 points. Players were substituted early and often to give the backups some playing time. Things started getting serious in the fourth game, an 11-0 win over Penn State. Virginia was taken down by a 12-0 score. Dickinson College was walloped in Harrisburg 36-0 in the first meeting between the teams in four years. Some bad blood had developed when Warner was coaching the Indians, but that seemed to be behind them at this point. Fumbles doomed the Indians to a 6-0 defeat at the hands of Penn. That game was followed by a 23-11 loss to Harvard in the mud. The following Saturday, the Indians beat the Cadets at West Point 6-5 in an historic game made possible only by permission of the War Department. This was the first time the Indians met "the soldiers" on an athletic field and they prevailed. This game, the ninth of the year, must have been considered the last regular season game because Coach Woodruff left the team at that time. He did not accompany them on their extended trip to Ohio, Western Pennsylvania and Washington, DC. Carlisle played five games in fifteen days against three college teams and two independent teams. They lost to the independents, Canton and Massillon, and beat Cincinnati, Washington and Jefferson, and Georgetown. After the Georgetown game, Chauncey's college playing days were over. He was a varsity starter from 1897 through 1905. Few other players could make such a claim. He was also one of the few Carlisle stars to never play for or assist Pop Warner. Warner arrived during his first year at Haskell, returned to Cornell after the 1903 season, and didn't return to Carlisle until 1907.

Barely two weeks after the end of football season, a basketball team was organized to represent the school and Archiquette was elected team captain. This was Carlisle's first formal attempt to officially field a team for the new sport. Previously, basketball had just been played regularly on campus and irregularly off-campus. Chauncey's return must have had something to do with this move; it's not clear if he coached the team or was just its captain. Physical Director Alfred Venne was in charge of the gymnasium and, in this capacity, may have served as coach. When James Naismith wrote, in *Basketball: Its Origins and Development*, "Carlisle was the first Indian school to play basketball...," he surely meant as an intra-mural sport. He also had an explanation why they took to it so well:

> "I have talked to several coaches of Indian teams and have found that coaching a team of Indian boys presents several problems that are not found among white boys. One coach told me that he had several good players who would not take part in the sport for fear of ridicule, and that some of the boys felt it inexcusable to make a mistake. They would not run this chance before a group of people. Besides, the Indian teams are usually made up of comparatively small men. This fact is a distinct handicap to them; but their ability to move quickly and

their art of deception overcome the disadvantage of their height, so that wherever these teams play they are assured of a large crowd of spectators."

Shortly after Christmas, a series of intra-mural basketball games were played between the classes: Seniors vs. Juniors and Sophomores vs. Freshmen. The Senior girls played a game against the Junior girls. The girls were more enthusiastic toward the game when women's rules were followed. Part of the New Year's festivities was a game between the varsity and the Sophomore boys. That two Junior boys were first string varsity players likely influenced the choice of opponents.

Carlisle's first, official intercollegiate basketball game was played at Lehigh University on January 20, 1906 with a large crowd present due to the fact that all Carlisle's players were well known football players. Frank Mt. Pleasant was surely a drawing card. The Indians lost 32-19 due to a lack of teamwork. The next week's practices were devoted to improving teamwork. A week later, when they hosted Muhlenburg College, Charlie Wahoo was on the floor. Carlisle prevailed 105-4. Their tight defense allowed the visitors to take few shots. The season ended on March 6 with a victory over Susquehanna University. The varsity basketball team went 7-6; not bad for a new team.

That spring, like most springs, found Chauncey on the baseball diamond, but this year he was in a Carlisle uniform. His surroundings weren't too strange because some of his fellow football and basketball teammates were also on that team.

Immediately after graduation, Wilson Charles got married in a most elaborate affair. Chauncey served as one of the groomsmen. Instead of competing in Annual Class Contest on April 30, as members of the staff, he and Siceni Nori judged the field events. After spending much of the summer as an outfielder for the school's baseball team, in August he departed for Pawhuska in the brand new state of Oklahoma, where he had a position as clerk at the Osage Agency.

There is no record of his returning to Carlisle but he kept in touch for a while. School records show that he responded to questionnaires in 1907, 1909, 1910 and 1911, but only copies of his 1907 and 1909 responses still exist. From these responses, we can learn a few things. He was promoted to Stenographer around August 1906 and was making $900 a year in 1909. In addition, he was provided furnished quarters at the Osage Agency and still owned his allotment back in Wisconsin. His answer to Question 11: Have you done anything for the betterment of your people?; was revealing. "I have not been among my people for eighteen years, and for a few days visit each time. Therefore I could not do them any good nor any harm." Clearly, he meant his own people to be the Oneidas.

He was still single, living in Pawhuska and working at the Osage Agency in September 1918 when he registered for the WWI draft. The 1920 census listed his parents and him as having been born in New York rather than Wisconsin, but that doesn't seem likely. It also listed his residence as in what must have been a large rooming house or hotel run by the widow Rhoda Sweeney Scott. They married in 1923. The 1924 Oneida census listed him as married but didn't list Rhoda, probably because she was white and not a member of the tribe. She died in 1930. USGenWeb archives for the Pawhuska Cemetery include both Chauncey and Rhoda Sweeney Archiquette, but no others of that family name. A 1926 newspaper article titled "Vanishing Americans Fade Out of Sport" said that Chauncey "has not been heard from, or of, for lo, these many, many moons. Like Metoxen, his famed teammate, he left without leaving a forwarding address." That wasn't exactly true. He left a forwarding address but the school where he left it was closed in 1918.

Chauncey Archiquette

Chauncey likely stayed active in sports after moving to Pawhuska but his best days were surely behind him or were after being there a few years. He was too old to play on the Oorang Indians and probably for the Hominy Indians, but may have assisted with coaching that team when his friend, Pete Hauser, coached them. But there is no evidence to support that.

He lived in Pawhuska until his death in 1949. For a time Pete Hauser lived with Rhoda and him, and they remained friends until Hauser's untimely death in an automobile accident at which Chauncey was present.

Charles Baird

Charles E. Baird first arrived at Carlisle on January 4, 1913 at age 17. In July when he was on an outing period at Bridgeville, New Jersey, he ran away and was dropped by the school. He was readmitted on October 24 for a three-year enrollment. Things must have gone better for him this time. He joined the band and football team. He didn't get into any varsity games but did play for the Scrubs in their scoreless 1915 season opener against Mercersburg Academy. While playing on the Scrubs or Reserves, as newspapers called them, may not sound like much of an achievement, something to keep in mind is that over 100 boys tried out for the Carlisle varsity in 1915. Charles again played right end when the Reserves lost to Conway Hall 6-0. The 64-0 drubbing by the Lebanon Valley College Reserves was unexpected. They scored against Blooms-

Name:	Charles E. Baird	Nickname:
DOB:	11/23/1895	Height:
Weight:		Age: 17
Parents:	Cornelius Baird Jr. Ida Baird	Home: Oneida, WI
Early Schooling:	Oneida Boarding School	
Later Schooling:	Ford Motor Company Apprenticeship	

burg Normal but lost 20-7 with Baird still at right end. With football season over, he turned to other things.

In January 1916, he, Joseph Denny, and Freeman Parkhurst left to work at Bethlehem Steel. Denny and Baird were soloists in the Carlisle band and expected to play in the company's band. Charles sent word back to Carlisle "...that he enjoys his work and his home with the good eats." At the end of the school year with his enrollment completed, Charles returned to his home in Wisconsin. The Acting Superintendent wrote Charles's father to tell him to expect Charles to arrive by train in Green Bay. He also stated:

> "As Charles will have the opportunity to prepare for selection to go to the Ford Motor Company's factory in Detroit, Michigan, it is hoped he will return here within a very few weeks to resume his work and studies. He has made so excellent a record here that nothing should be allowed to interfere with the continuation of his school work."

Charles returned and was selected for the Ford apprenticeship program. Some complained that football boys were given priority over other students for this opportunity. The list of those selected includes many football players. He was soon on the list of those apprentices who were making $2.72 a day and sending one-fourth of this to their school savings account.

The U. S. instituted a draft following entry into World War I in the spring of 1917. Charles classified himself as "Natural born - Indian" and as a "Student - Ford Motor Co." on his Registration Card. For prior military service rank, he entered "Musician" and "Band" for the branch. He enter 3½ years for the length of service and "Carlisle Tg School - Penna." For the nation or state. He might have been angling to be assigned to a band.

Charles's student file included several communications between Ford, Carlisle, and the Oneida Reservation concerning finances. Most of them had to do with sending portions of Charles's earnings to his parents. His father, a farmer, had been unable to work for some time, so the funds transfers were approved but were to be sent to his mother.

According to the June 30, 1917 fiscal-year-end report, Charles Baird earned $776.60 for the year. To have earned that much, he must have completed his apprenticeship and made $5.00 a day for a significant period of time.

Henry Lange wrote about his and Charles's experiences:

> "We were recruited from the Ford Motor Company for expert repairmen to do field work and to ship as soon as the ambulances were ready, you can see we don't expect to be in camp many 'moons' before we see active service in France."

Ford supplied thousands of ambulance built on Model T chassis for the Army and Red Cross. Skilled mechanics would be needed to keep them in service. Hence the recruiting at the factory. As members of the U. S. Corps, Ford Repair Unit, they were stationed at Camp Hill, Virginia, an embarkation site located at Newport News, before shipping off to France. They were able to see the Carlisle-Hampton Institute basketball game played in nearby Hampton, Virginia in February 1918.

Six nurses stand in front of a Model T ambulance "Hunka Tin"

HUNKA TIN

"Hunka Tin" was a poem written as a parody on Rudyard Kipling's "Gunga Din." It appeared in the *American Field Service Bulletin* during WWI and is said to have even used in Ford dealers' advertising throughout the United States.
The final stanza of the parody reads:

Yes, Tin, Tin, Tin,
You exasperating puzzle, Hunka Tin,
I've abused you and I've flayed you,
But, by Henry Ford who made you,
You are better than a Packard, Hunka tin.

After the war, Charles returned to Detroit. Whether he took his old job with Ford or not isn't known with certainty. The 1920 census lists him as a repairman working at an auto factory. At first repairman seem like an unusual job title for someone working at an assembly plant. But with hundreds of cars coming off the production line each day, some will have problems that need to be corrected. He would have developed specialized skills with repairing Model T ambulances in the field Ford would have found most useful.

In 1923, he married Agnes Day Bird (sometimes Daybird). Agnes and her sister were Ottawas from Harbor Springs, Michigan who arrived at Carlisle on September 29, 1917 as members of the Junior Class. They were transferred to Haskell Institute when Carlisle closed in 1918. Charles may have met her when he visited Carlisle in December 1917. They could have corresponded when he was in the Army and waited to marry until he became better situated financially in Michigan. They were married in Detroit by a Justice of the Peace, John O. McKinley. Fred and Willa Skenandore stood up for them.

According to the 1930 Census, Charles and Agnes rented an apartment on Sharon Avenue and had a boarder, Ernest Duckett, but no children. Charles worked in auto repair at an auto plant. The Model

A was in production then and an experienced mechanic like Baird would have been valuable to Ford.

He died on April 12, 1931 due to Chronic Endocarditis which may have been brought about by Tuberculosis, which was prevalent at the time. According to the Certificate of Death, he was living at 21 Midland in Highland Park and working at Ford. He had probably worked there all along.

Wilson Charles

The details of Wilson Charles's early life are somewhat vague. The first record of his existence that could be found was the 1885 census of the Oneida Agency which listed him as being six years of age. His father, Julius Charles, may have been of mixed blood and, according to Susan G. Daniel's research, died in 1884. His mother, Sophia Metoxen Charles, was a 23-year-old widow with three children. Besides Wilson, there was 5-year-old Elias and 3-year-old Josephine. These ages are approximations at best because birthdates for people of that period are questionable. Most of the censuses put Wilson's year of birth at 1879. However, when he registered for the World War I draft, he wrote March 10, 1881 as his date of birth. That date is possible, but squeezes the births of three children into four years. On the other hand, he may

Name:	Wilson Beleves Charles	Nickname:	Chicken Legs
DOB:	3/10/1879	Height:	5'9"
Weight:	150 lbs.	Age:	20
Parents:	Julius Charles Sophia Metoxen Charles	Home:	DePere, WI
Early Schooling:	Oneida Boarding School? Haskell Institute?		
Later Schooling:			

have shaved off a couple of years to make himself eligible for the draft. The family disappeared from the rolls after the 1885 entry. Perhaps censuses were not taken in those years. Wilson showed up next on the 1892 roll listed with Hulda Doxtator Wheelock Charles, his paternal grandmother and the grandmother of Dennison and James Wheelock, the famous Carlisle bandmasters, through a previous marriage. His grandfather, David Charles, appears to have died sometime after the 1885 census and before 1892. Wilson's siblings were listed with their maternal grandparents, Abram and Jerusha Metoxen on the 1892 roll. Josephine Charles's relationship was adopted. Elias Metoxen was listed as a son. The 1902 census implies that both may have been considered Metoxens and may have been adopted. Wilson and Huldah were listed together for several years, but around the turn of the twentieth century, they were listed as living at the Oneida Indian Boarding School. However, it is unlikely that he attended that school or, if he did, not for long. One newspaper account stated that he attended Haskell Institute before entering Carlisle.

The July 12, 1901 issue of *The Red Man and Helper* listed Wilson Charles among those who had gone home recently. Because students were not usually allowed to return home before the end of an enrollment and that enrollments at that time were generally for five years, he first came to Carlisle around 1896. He was old enough to have come much earlier and very well could have. Unfortunately, his Carlisle student file as well as those of his siblings have been lost. Without them, we can't know for sure when they enrolled. Being orphans, it is reasonable to assume that they were enrolled when young. The lack of records makes it necessary to surmise their activities from later statements. In September, he returned for another enrollment as a Freshman.

Wilson's name started showing up more frequently in the school newspaper in 1901 when he vied for fullback position on the varsity football team: "Charles is rather light, but he is a good punter and the best dropkicker on the field." Wilson made the team but not the first team. He spent the season on the bench until the last quarter of the last game—a trouncing by Columbia University at the Polo Grounds in New York. With the Indians losing 40-0, he finally got to play and made the most of it. In addition to making good yardage on line plunges, he scored the Indians only two touchdowns in the game. Those were made using the wing shift which completely befuddled the Columbians. Football season was over but he didn't while away his time waiting for next year.

Wilson Charles had a pleasing baritone voice and used it to sing solos and in groups as well as to orate. In May, he entertained the faculty by singing in a mixed quarter with Edith Bartlett, Delfina Jacques and Walter Comah. He, Philip Tousey, Phineas Wheelock, and Wallace Denny closed the program with a humorous dialog. A week later, he performed well in the annual inter-class track meet, placing third in the 100-yard dash, second in the broad jump,

second in the 120-yard hurdles, tied for first in the high jump, and first in the 220-yard dash. He did almost as well in a dual meet with Dickinson College a week later, winning both the broad jump and high jump events, placing second in the 120-yard hurdles, and coming in third in the shotput. He didn't do nearly as well in the dual meet with Penn State, placing second in both high jump and broad jump.

Coach Warner remarked about Wilson's improvement in pre-season football practices. He played quarterback in the first half of the Lebanon Valley College game to start the 1902 season. His brother, Elias played fullback for the Printers team. Wilson was shifted to right halfback for the Gettysburg College game. Newspaper reporters dubbed him the "hero" of that game for his fine running and punting. As the season progressed, he played some at fullback, some at quarterback, but mostly at right halfback. He wasn't a star yet, but he was a regular.

Wilson sang in "the school quartet" with Monroe Coulon, Alfred Venne and Henry Tatiyopi. Their performance during Christmas week received notice in the school newspaper. In January, as a member of the Invincible Debating Society, he sang in a quintet that was received so well the audience demanded an encore. He also sang a solo that showed off the depths of his vocal range. In March, he serenaded them with "My Old Kentucky Home." Early in the New Year he played on the Sophomores' basketball team—Carlisle didn't have a varsity squad yet—along with Joel Cornelius, Wallace Denny, Randolph Hill, and Thomas Gardner. Charles was the team's captain. He was also captain of the school's track team that year. In a pre-season indoor meet to give new team members an opportunity to compete with the old ones, he won the 35-yard dash and shotput events, tied for first in the high jump, and finished second in the 35-yard high hurdles.

After commencement, Wilson was promoted to the Junior Class and was elected Class Treasurer. He decorated the blackboard in the Junior room with a drawing that was "artistic and highly appreciated by his classmates." The Invincibles then elected him Assistant Critic. He helped win a banner for the school and a gold watch for himself at the

Penn Relay Carnival as a member of the winning relay team along with Wallace Denny, James Johnson, and Frank Mt. Pleasant. Their time would have been better if Johnson and Mt. Pleasant had been pushed to exert themselves. As it was, the Indians won by 20 yards. Wilson won more hardware at the annual class meet in late Apri: a handsome watch fob for earning more points for his class than any other competitor. His classmates also gave him a gold medal engraved with "Class contest, 1903." In addition to winning or placing in several events, he set school records in the high jump and the broad jump. Wilson also did well in the meets against other schools that spring, often leading his team in points scored. Against Bucknell, he broke his own school broad jump record. When spring ended, it was time for summer outings.

It's not known where Wilson Charles spent the summer of 1903, but New Jersey would be a good guess. *The Red Man and Helper* reported that Wilson, Truman Doxtator, and Joseph Baker visited the Zoological Gardens, Independence Hall, Academy of Fine Arts, and Academy of Natural Science in Philadelphia on their way back to Carlisle at summer's end. Truman Doxtator worked at Beacon-by-the-sea in Point Pleasant, New Jersey as did Wilson's brother, Elias, which would have made hooking up with them logical. In the fall, Wilson was elected Corresponding Secretary of the Junior Class.

Charles earned his first football letter playing right halfback and fullback that year. He did better at halfback because he was small for a fullback. The football trips gave him something to share with his classmates. After the Georgetown game, William White, Joseph Baker, and he told their fellow Juniors some interesting facts about Washington. On the trip west to Utah and California, Wilson wrote his teacher, Miss Wood, a letter to share with his classmates. Later on the trip, he wrote:

> "It did not seem to me that Christmas was anywhere near while we were in San Francisco. Everything there is so beautiful. The flowers that we saw in Pennsylvania in August are to be seen in California now, while in Penn-

sylvania there is good skating. I understand that the weather doesn't change much from winter to summer. To-day [sic] it is like summer and so warm we would rather stay in the shade than out in the sun. I have learned much about this country."

In the winter of 1904, Wilson Charles probably played on the Juniors Class basketball team but no team roster has been found. His brother, Elias, worked as a printer in town for *The Evening Sentinel*. Wilson continued his singing with a solo for the football banquet, at which he got his first letter for football. Charles also sang in a quartet for a school assembly. An encore was requested, but they inexplicably did not respond. Perhaps, they had not prepared another song. He also served as President of the Invincibles. In the spring, he pitched for the school baseball team, racking up several wins. At the 5th Annual Class Contest, Wilson scored the most points of any contestant by winning the 100-yard dash, 120-yard hurdles, and the broad jump and coming in second in the shot put and high jump. Then a member of the Senior Class, he scored all of their points. His brother Elias finished fourth in the 120-yd hurdles. Wilson even found time to compete for the track team. In the meet with Penn State he placed second in the 120-yd hurdles and broad jump. He also placed second in the 120-yd hurdles against Bucknell. Not bad considering he hadn't spent much time training for track because of his baseball commitment.

Elias Charles took a short vacation to "visit his old country home near Trenton." He returned to work half-days at *The Evening Sentinel* and attend school the other half. Due to the lack of a student file and mention in the school paper, all that is known about Wilson's summer is that he returned in time for football season. Playing baseball for a community or minor league team would be a distinct possibility.

Football was a little frustrating for him in 1904. All the previous year's starters returned except the quarterback and fullback. Joe Baker and Archie Libby were great candidates for the quarterback position.

That left team captain Arthur Sheldon with one choice of positions for Wilson: fullback. Coach Rogers explained his dilemma:

> "The position of full-back, however, will be a problem, as all the available men with a sufficient amount of weight have been compelled to play in the line and this leaves a wealth of light material to select from. Captain Sheldon, who played regularly at half-back last year, is being tried out at this position. He is the heaviest of the backfield candidates, but does not seem to take to the position quite as readily as he does to half-back. Charles is also trying for the position. He is very light, but is developing into a speedy man and can boot the leather in great style. Nephew and La Roque are also developing promise, especially La Roque who is a new Indian just from the wilds of Minnesota. La Roque has fair weight and can develop speed, but has yet a lot to learn about the full-back position."

Early into the season, Coach Rogers again commented on Charles's play:

> "Considerable attention has been paid to the kicking department of the game and to the catching of punts. Captain Sheldon, Charles, and Tomahawk have done the punting. Charles has shown up the best, sending off long spirals at distances from forty to sixty yards. Sheldon is practicing faithfully in trying to overcome some bad faults. Tomahawk's punts are erratic."

Rogers also discussed the continuing backfield situation. Note that he had settled on a quarterback and did not rotate that position:

"Three sets of backs are being used and developed. One set, composed of Captain Sheldon, Hendricks, and La Roque have been given the preference because of their weight and experience, but in fact have not shown that they can play any better than a set made up of Charles, Saul, and Whitecrow, nor of the other set composed of Fischer, Nephew, and Doxtator. There is not much choice between these sets and all are being given a good tryout. There will be plenty of good backs."

Wilson Charles got enough playing time to score a few touchdowns and letter again, but wasn't a big star that year. That the 1904 team was a good one with a lot of talent was brought into focus when the game against Haskell Institute the Saturday after Thanksgiving was added to the schedule. The Thanksgiving Day game against Ohio State immediately became less important and was relegated to the Second Team. Wilson played right halfback part of the game and fullback the rest of it. He also kicked four goals after touchdown—extra points in modern parlance—in the 23-0 outclassing of the Buckeyes. That he didn't get into the Haskell game wasn't as negative as it might at first seem. Coaches Ed Rogers, Bemus Pierce, and Hawley Pierce suited up for the game and played much of it. Bemus started at right halfback and Hawley at fullback. Their availability moved Wilson down the depth charts for both positions. Brother Elias spent his Thanksgiving Day on the football field playing fullback for the Printers, occasionally slamming through the Carpenters' line for long gains.

He didn't spend all of his time that semester emersed in athletics. As part of the entertainment for the Annual Football Banquet, Wilson sang in a quartet with Alfred M. Venne, Ignatius Ironroad, and Walter A. Komal. After completing their planned performance, they sang two encores and finished with "College Chum." He also sang solos for the

Junior Varsity Reception and as part of a quartet with Ignatius Ironroad, Adam Fischer, and Fritz Hendricks.

Elizabeth Knudsen

In October he and Elizabeth Knudsen, Yurok from California and a member of the Class of 1903, won the cake for best marching at a reception held by the Susan Longstreth Literary Society. She was considered by some to be the prettiest girl on campus. Having already graduated, it wasn't clear exactly what she was pursuing at that time except, perhaps, Wilson. She may have been enrolled in the normal school or commercial program or could have been employed by the school. In February, she led the large girls' meeting, which might mean that she was still a student. Also, she remained active with the Susans.

Wilson graduated in March of 1905. At some point after that, he became an employee of the school, most likely as an assistant in the carriage-making shop. That spring he didn't play baseball or run track for the school, but Elias ran the hurdles while filling in as the acting foreman in the printing office during Mr. Baird's absence. Elizabeth Knudsen sang a solo for the Susans in the spring and, in late July, visited her country parents in Beverly, New Jersey. Wilson spent his vacation pitching for Green Bay in the Wisconsin League. At summer's end, he returned to Carlisle to vie for a position on the 1905 football team.

Charles played part of the first game, a warm-up against P. R. R. YMCA of Columbia, Pennsylvania, at fullback. Soon Wilson was platooning at right halfback. Later in the season he played some at left halfback. He didn't get into the Army or Massillon games but, later on the long road trip, starred against Cincinnati by scoring a touchdown on a 90-yard run, kicking a field goal, and making three extra points. He didn't play against Washington and Jefferson but had a field day against Georgetown. Only playing in the second half, he scored a touchdown, kicked a field goal, and made five extra points in the 76-0 romp. This year, he got enough playing time to letter.

Shortly after commencement, Wilson Charles married Elizabeth Knudsen in an elaborate ceremony officiated by Rev. Alexander McMillan of the Episcopal Church in Carlisle. Over 1,000 people attended, requiring it to be held in the school auditorium. Major Mercer gave the bride away as was the custom at the school. Males participating in the ceremony wore their dress uniforms. Wilson wore the rank of captain and Quartermaster of the Superintendent's staff. Elias Charles, who had just graduated, served as best man before leaving Carlisle to take a course in electro-typing. Frank Mt. Pleasant, Genus Baird, Chauncey Archiquette, Wallace Denny, Charles Roy, and William Gardner were the groomsmen. Ida Nori was Elizabeth's matron-of-honor. Josephine Charles, Minnie Rice, Rose McFarland, Stacey Beck, Bertha Dennis, and Mary Runnels were her bridesmaids. The Carlisle Indian School orchestra played the wedding march from Tannhauser as the processional and Mendelssohn's Wedding March for the recessional. News services distributed coverage of the wedding across the country. After a wedding trip to West Point and other points of interest in the east, the Wilsons set up housekeeping on the school campus.

Wilson Charles went out for baseball in the spring of 1906 but not track. He twirled some games with success before heading home to Wisconsin on vacation. According to a later account in *The Arrow*, the southpaw pitched again for the Green Bay team, winning a 13-inning game from Wausau 3-2. He also held Eau Claire to six hits to win the team's final home game 5-3. Josephine spent her summer at her country home in Morton, Pennsylvania. Upon her return to school in September 1906, she cooked for the athletes' training table.

Wilson played football again but mostly as a back-up. He did start the Cincinnati game and played well again. This time he was credited with a number of long punts and sharp tackling. He didn't get enough playing time to letter in 1906. He continued to work as assistant coach-maker until late March, when he reported to Danville, Virginia for spring training with the Trenton team of the Tri-State League. In mid-April of 1907, he was back twirling for the Green Bay club. After baseball season was over, he changed his pattern by not returning to Carlisle. Instead, he coached a high school football team in the Green Bay area. Elias spent the fall in the country recuperating from an unnamed illness.

According to an article in the January 3, 1908 edition of *The Arrow*, Wilson had been offered a college coaching job for the upcoming football season. The May 30, 1908 issue of *Sporting Life* listed him as having signed with Butler, Pennsylvania of the Ohio-Pennsylvania League for the current baseball season. That October, he wrote *The Carlisle Arrow* that he was at Haskell Institute where he was employed in the wagon shops in addition to assisting with the coaching of the football team. His sister, Josephine, Carlisle '08, wrote that she was also in government service, working as an assistant matron at Wahpeton Indian School in North Dakota. The October 7, 1910 issue of *The Carlisle Arrow* indicated that Josephine was "getting along finely with her work in DePere, Wisconsin." The 1910 Federal Census listed her as living with her cousin, Dennison Wheelock, and working as a servant, thus no longer with the government. Whether she worked for the Wheelocks or someone else was unclear. Regardless, she was soon back in the Indian Service. *The Carlisle Arrow* of June 7, 1912 reported that she was again employed in the Indian Service working at Hoopa, California. It was there she apparently met her husband. Around 1914, Josephine married Eric Swanson, a woodsman who was not listed on the Oneida roll perhaps because his father was from Sweden and his mother wasn't Oneida. They lived in Humboldt County, California where they soon had two sons and two daughters.

According to the 1910 census, Elias Charles was back in Wisconsin living with Wilson. His note from DePere, Wisconsin that was published in the May 5, 1912 edition of *The Carlisle Arrow* tells us more about what he was doing:

> "As I am one in Carlisle's great family, I want to express my gratitude for what Mother Carlisle has done for me. I have had many experiences since I left the school. For two years I worked at my trade of printing until sickness overtook me. I left the city life and went to work on a farm nine miles from Carlisle, where I worked two more years. I then accepted a position as industrial teacher at the Red Lake Indian School, Minnesota, but to my disappointment the climate did not agree with me. I then went to the lumber camps. Now I am farming here."

Elias Charles had married Lena Schenandoah (Skenandore?) around 1910 and had a son, Paul, in 1911. By 1917, Paul was dead and his parents appear to have split up. Elias lived alone in Wisconsin until he was 50. He then moved to California to live with his sister and her family.

The 1910 census listed Wilson Charles as living in Oneida (the town) in Outagamie County, Wisconsin and working as a carpenter. Elizabeth worked as a dressmaker. Elias was listed as a member of the household. Wilson and Elizabeth had two children. Edna was born in 1907 in Pennsylvania and Wilson Junior was born in 1909 in Wisconsin. According to tribal rolls and Wilson Senior's WWI draft registration, the two didn't share a middle name. Wilson Jr.'s middle initial was D whereas Wilson Sr.'s middle name was Beleves. Wilson Jr. was better known as Buster.

A 1914 press release from Carlisle that was picked up across the nation stated that Wilson Sr. was "instrumental in developing athletics in the government school at Toma, Minn." He was likely working at Tomah Industrial School in Tomah, Wisconsin because that is where he worked as an industrial teacher when he registered for the WWI draft on September 12, 1918. The Charleses moved to Flandreau Indian School in Moody County, South Dakota, probably in the early 1920s, where Wilson worked as an advisor and Elizabeth was a matron. Some newspaper articles also credited him with being athletic director. They returned to Wisconsin later in the decade.

In February 1930, Wilson, who had pitched for the Green Bay team in 1927, began putting together a team of Indians that would tour the country.

Buster followed in his father's athletic footsteps and, being larger physically, had even greater success. He reputedly won All-State honors in football in 1926 and 1927 and the state championships in both high jump and broad jump in 1927. After high school, Buster enrolled at Haskell Institute in Lawrence, Kansas. Lone Star Dietz, his coach at Haskell, thought he might become another Jim Thorpe. Buster finished third in the decathlon at the 1928 Olympic try-outs in Philadelphia. He took first place in the first five events of the decathlon at the 1929 Kansas Relays. The next day, Oklahoma Olympic star bettered his best mark in somehow nosing out Charles, who had won a total of six of the individual events. In addition to having an outstanding career at Haskell,

Buster echoed Thorpe by competing in the decathlon in the 1932 Los Angeles Olympics. He led at the end of the first day with the most points in the first five events. On the second day, his teammate from Kansas, Jim Bausch, smashed the Olympic record for the decathlon to bits. Buster finished fourth.

After graduating from Haskell Institute in 1932, Buster attended the University of New Mexico. Wilson Sr. and his mother joined him there. After Buster married and took a job in Oklahoma, Wilson and Elizabeth remained in New Mexico at Crown Point near Gallup. She died two years later. Wilson remarried to Anna Hale, Pottawatamie from Kansas, before 1940. Both were working for the Indian Service, he as

Oneida's own

Buster Charles

an electrical engineer and her as a matron. In 1950, both were still working. Wilson died in 1952 at 71 years of age.

Casper Cornelius

Casper Cornelius first arrived at Carlisle on August 28, 1897 at twelve years of age. During that five-year enrollment, He primarily trained on farming and worked on farms during his outing periods. However, he worked at harness making part of his first term at Carlisle. At the end of his enrollment in September 1902, he returned home. In December 1903, he started a second enrollment. This time he trained as a blacksmith and again went on outings to farms.

He made the varsity football team in 1906 because he is included in team photos that were circulated to newspapers across the country. However, playing time was hard to get because the competition was fierce as the team was loaded with talented players.

His name first appeared in print in school publications in 1906 when he joined the Invincible Debating Society. Casper was active with the Invincibles the remainder of his time at Carlisle. He joined the

Name:	Casper E. Cornelius	Nickname:	Cap
DOB:	4/16/1885	Height:	5'11"
Weight:	161 lbs.	Age:	17
Parents:	Thomas Gray Cornelius Sarah John Cornelius	Home:	De Pere, WI
Early Schooling:	Oneida Indian School		
Later Schooling:	Chilocco Indian School		

YMCA in February 1907 and was elected janitor. He and John Waterman attended the state convention in Allentown in March. Casper played one of Miles Standish's soldiers in the comic opera "Priscilla" that was put on by Carlisle students in April. In July he attended the Northfield Conference in Massachusetts. A highlight of the trip was an all-night steamship ride from New York City to New London, Connecticut. Early his last year at Carlisle, he wrote that he wanted to be a clerk in a store and wished to get an education in business. Upon returning from the conference, Casper left Carlisle for good, his enrollment completed.

He didn't stay in Wisconsin long, if he ever returned home at all. A reason for that may have been his 25-acre allotment was, in his opinion, a swamp that couldn't be cultivated. If he didn't own other land, this would have been the parcel he had sold in June 1906 to J. V. Humphreys for $900. He attended Chilocco Indian School from August 1907 to May 1908, taking a course in printing. In the winter, he played on the Chilocco basketball team.

During the baseball season he played on a traveling team, the Oxford [Nebraska] Indians. *The Carlisle Arrow* reported in November 1908 that he was working in Kansas City. A week later, it corrected that to Arkansas City, Kansas where he worked packing flour at Arkansas City Milling Company for a salary of $48 per month. In 1910 he tried out for the Blackwell, Oklahoma baseball team. He apparently made the team and found employment in that town.

In November 1911, Casper wrote *The Carlisle Arrow* that he was employed as second cook at Oxford Hotel in Coldwater, Kansas making $35 per week and that he enjoyed "...nothing more than to read *The Carlisle Arrow* and it often makes him wish he were back at Carlisle."

In May 1912 he wrote Superintendent Friedman that he was working for Electric Light and Waterworks Construction Co. in Englewood in southwestern Kansas. In December he was operating a tailoring, cleaning, and pressing business. "I only regret that the town is not any larger." That business didn't last very long because he was farming at Red Rock, Oklahoma in 1914.

In 1915, he played baseball for the Blackwell, Oklahoma team. He joined the fire company, and worked at local industrial plants. In the winter, he tried out for the local basketball team. The next July, he wrote *The Arrow* to have his subscription shifted from Bucklin, Kansas to De Pere, Wisconsin because he was going there while his mother was ill. He also wrote about being in the restaurant business. The business was doing well and he planned on returning to it. How long he stayed isn't clear. His mother was still alive in June 1916 but not in June 1917 because her name disappeared from the tribal roll. She may have died in late 1916 because Casper tried out for the Blackwell Athletic Club basketball squad in December and was expected to make the first team.

In late-September 1918, Casper was one of 168 men listed as about to be drafted into the Army to fight World War I. On November 11, he and eleven others were sworn in and were scheduled to be put on Train 12 for Fort Riley, Kansas that evening. However, the Armistice was signed well before the train was to leave. The local draft board chairman received orders to proceed with entrainment as if the armistice hadn't been signed. Shortly before the train was to leave, new orders were received. All National Army movements were to stop and the new inductees were sent home. How long Casper served isn't clear but it couldn't have been long.

An August 1919 newspaper stated that Casper had married Tina Maine on the 6th in Bucklin, Kansas. A later newspaper article reported that he had married Pina M. Lane on September 3. The next January, they were living in a house Casper owned outright in Reno, Kansas. He was working as a harness maker. She was the bookkeeper for a doctor.

In November 1920 a parcel he owned in the Town of Oneida was listed as being up for sale by the county for unpaid taxes of $8.10. He must have paid the taxes just in time because the property was listed again a few years later. This cycle was repeated several times in the next few decades.

In 1930, Casper was a boarder living with Luther and Inez Craycraft in Bucklin, Kansas. He was divorced and worked as a carpenter, probably building houses.

The obituary for Casper's father, Thomas Gray Cornelius, who died in 1936, listed Caser's address as unknown. He may not have had any contact with his family since his mother died.

Luther Craycraft died in 1937, leaving Inez as a widow with at least four children still at home. Casper remarried in 1939 to Inez Craycraft and soon moved to Green Forest, Arkansas where he worked as a laborer on construction projects in 1940. By 1950, they moved to a farm near Green Forest.

In October 1961, he was ticketed for "improper turning" in Claremore, Oklahoma. Casper died on November 8, 1969 in Berryville, Arkansas at the age of 84 as the result of some sort of accident involving a sewer. The handwriting on his death certificate was difficult to decipher. His heart blockage may have been a contributing factor. His usual occupation was listed as carpenter and his wife was Inez Alspach Cornelius. He was buried in Glenwood Cemetery in Green Forest, Arkansas.

Joel Cornelius

Joel Cornelius arrived at Carlisle on August 28, 1891 for a five-year enrollment. His age was recorded as 13. However, he may have been 14 or 15. Dates of birth weren't recorded well in those days, particularly on the reservations. He later gave his date of birth as August 22, 1877 on his WWI draft registration. Although having had 12 months of schooling prior to coming, he was placed in the First Grade classroom. His trade was listed as Clothing Room. He started going out on outings the following summer, most likely to do farm work.

Playing quarterback, Joel captained the Second Team in its 40-0 victory over Carlisle High School on Thanksgiving Day 1898. In 1900, Joel got some playing time at fullback in the varsity's 45-0 annihilation of Gettysburg College and the Second Team's 12-6 defeat of the Harrisburg YMCA team. An early-November outbreak of measles caused the football squad to relocate to Pine Grove Park while the school was quarantined. On the evening before the annual game with

Name:	Joel O. Cornelius	Nickname:	
DOB:	8/22/1876	Height:	5'6½"
Weight:	153 lbs.	Age:	23
Parents:	William O. Cornelius Esther Cornelius	Home:	West De Pere, WI
Early Schooling:	Oneida Indian School		
Later Schooling:	Heidelberg University		

Penn, the passenger train the team was riding to Philadelphia on collided with a freight train that was parked on the tracks at the Mechanicsburg station. The players weren't injured but were badly shaken up. They returned to Carlisle and took an early train to Philadelphia the morning of the game. The wreck and its aftermath probably affected their play in the 16-6 loss in which Cornelius didn't play.

Joel extended his first enrollment five additional years, waiting until July 1901 to return home. He returned with a group led by James Wheelock in September and started another five-year enrollment.

In February 1902 he was elected President of the Sophomore Class. In March, he was put in charge of Classroom 12 one morning due to Mrs. Cook's absence. He was demonstrating leadership qualities.

In the 1902 varsity game against Gettysburg, the team performed better in the second half when he, Dillon, Fischer, Wilson Charles, and Sheldon were substituted into the fray. "Cornelius [at quarterback] handled the ball like a veteran, but was careless in handling punts." He played quarterback again in the Bucknell game, a 16-0 loss. And again in the 50-0 drubbing of Bloomsburg State Normal School. Yet again against Cornell in the Indians' 10-6 win. Johnson was still out for the Susquehanna thrashing, so Joel started again.

Joel Cornelius

That winter, Joel played on the Sophomore Class's basketball team. He cut his enrollment short in February 1903 because he was needed at home to work the farm after his father died. *The Sentinel* described him as "the crack sub-quarter-back" when reporting his departure. Joel had bad luck in that he had to beat out Frank Hudson for playing time in his early years with the team and James Johnson in the later years. In April, *The Patriot-News* reported that he had taken a job at a Wisconsin Indian school. In September, he wrote that the job was as a fireman.

In early October of 1904 Joel joined the football squad for Heidelberg University in Tiffin, Ohio. Former Carlisle student Caleb Stickles, who was coaching Heidelberg, recruited him. Joel starred at right halfback in his first game with the team, a 85-0 pummeling of Lima Athletic Association. They needed more than Joel to beat the Medical College. Handicapped by injuries from the Medics game and playing against a line that averaged 200 pounds, they lost to Denison. He helped them bounce back against Fort Wayne Medical University. He helped out in the 5-0 win over Otterbein. Wittenberg played its best game against Heidelberg, defeating them 17-0.

Joel went home after the season ended and returned to play for Heidelberg again in 1905. *Cleveland Plain Dealer* mentioned him in its write up of the 12-0 loss to Western Reserve: "The star of the day's work was probably Cornelius, Heidelberg's right half. He frequently tackled for losses behind the line." Two weeks later he shifted to quarterback and scored the only touchdown in the 9-0 win over Otterbein. He replaced Brundage at quarterback for the second half against Lorain Athletic Association but returned to halfback against the Michigan Freshmen. Both were Heidelberg wins as was the rematch against Lorain A. A. a week later. Joel sat out the Denison loss, probably due to injury. He returned for the season-ending loss to Toledo Athletic Association. The team had so many injuries that Coach Sickles suited up at left end. Heidelberg went 6-4-0, due in some part to Joel's participation.

In 1906, he returned to farming full-time and married Leah Skenandoah on December 27 in an Episcopal ceremony. "[S]ince then I have been living on a small farm (30 acres) of land partly cleared and sone woods," he wrote to Superintendent Friedman in 1912.

In 1907 the government transferred 45 acres to Joel and he purchased 25 more from Carrie Webster. The next year he and Leah sold a parcel on the reservation to George School for $2,000.

By 1910, they had two daughters. In 1912, he wrote Superintendent Friedman about his life after leaving Carlisle. "I have three children and I should just like to see the day that they could attend the school of Carlisle or a school similar to it." He then inquired about bringing some children to Carlisle. Friedman responded that he would pay Joel's way if he found a group who wanted to come. There was no documentation of this ever happening.

On his WWI Draft Registration, he listed his birth year as 1877. It was 1876 on his marriage license. He may have been trying to appear younger and more virile for military duty.

In 1922 he was elected to the school board. He served as clerk for the board for many years.

In 1925, he debated with the Wide Awake Club unsuccessfully supporting the affirmative of "Women should build fires mornings."

By 1930, he and Leah had three daughters and two sons.

Joel died on July 14, 1941 at 65 after a long illness. He was survived by his widow, four sons, and three daughters. He was buried in the Episcopal Church cemetery.

Phillip Cornelius

Phillip Cornelius arrived at Carlisle on September 7, 1905 for a five-year enrollment. In December, he worked with some other boys in grading the muddy ground around the new chicken houses at the near farm. Mr. Leaman said they worked well and quietly without a word of complaint and with manly good will. He received good marks for both academics and conduct. In 1909 he joined the Capenter Shop, where he continued learning and working the rest of his time at the school. That year he also joined the Invincible Debating Society and participated in debates. After completing his five-year term in 1910, he returned for a three-year term of enrollment.

In 1911, he progressed into cabinet making and built a round table. He spent the summer working as a carpenter in Willow Grove, Pennsylvania. In September 1912, he took charge of the Carpentry Shop during Mr. Herr's illness. In December he and William Robinson built

Name:	Phillip Cornelius	Nickname:	
DOB:	1/22/1888	Height:	5' 7¼"
Weight:	135 pounds	Age:	16
Parents:	Isaac O. Cornelius Melissa Stevens Cornelius	Home: Clan:	West De Pere, WI Wolf
Early Schooling:	Oneida Boarding School		
Later Schooling:			

a stairway from the dining room to the sewing room on the second floor. That year he joined and played a leadership role in the YMCA while remaining active with the Invincibles. He was also elected as a Councilman for the Freshman Class. In the January 1913 opening exercises, he gave a recitation titled "Give Us Men." He was also promoted to Captain in charge of Troop C to march in the Presidential Inaugural Parade in Washington, DC.

In the spring 1907 Class Contest, Phillip finished third in the 220-yard hurdles behind Sundown and Thorpe. He made the varsity football team in 1908 and was in the back row of the team photo. In April 1909, he came in second in the first Handicap Track Meet quarter-mile run behind Friday. In 1910 he came in third, behind Twohearts and Morris. In May as a member of the Second Team in a meet against Harrisburg High and Conway Hall, he came in second in the 440-yard dash behind Martin. In the Orange Indoor Meet in 1911, Phillip won the 5-lap race. In the Annual Class Meet, he came in third in the 440-yard dash behind Welch and Martin and fourth in the half-mile run behind Priest, Arquette, and Shasbowobosh.

In the fall of 1911, as recognition of his leadership skills, Phillip was elected captain of the Second Team. In the winter at the Orange Indoor Meet, he won the relay with teammates Martin, Fox, and Tarbell. On Monday October 7, 1912, he finally got his name in printed game coverage. He played quarterback for the Reserves in their scoreless tie with Conway Hall the preceding Saturday. Reserves' games were seldom covered by the newspapers. Rarer yet was including the team line-ups for the games. The next week, he got his name in print again, this time for kicking the winning field goal against J. A. C. of Norristown. He received more print coverage for singing at Carlisle events than for football.

In February 1914, *The Carlisle Arrow* reported that Phillip had taken an assistant engineer position at Tomah Indian School in Wisconsin. In March, it reported that he had written Mr. Herr to inform him that he was employed as a carpentry instructor at Tomah.

He married Lena Ludwick, Oneida, on June 30, 1916. She had been a teacher before being married, likely at Tomah. When Phillip registered for the WWI draft in September 1918, he was working as a carpenter for Seims, Halmers & Schaffner in Superior, Wisconsin. He was married and claimed dependents.

In 1925 he was elected chief of the Wolf Clan. The 1928 Oneida Census listed Phillip as being married to Lena and having three daughters and a son. The 1930 Federal Census listed him as working as a carpenter for a contractor and renting a house at 505 Lincoln Avenue in Little Chute, Wisconsin. At some point, he was elected president of the Carpenters Union at Little Chute, No. 2244. He was also a member of Kaukauna Lodge 233 of Free and Accepted Masons.

The 1940 Federal Census listed him as a lock tender working for the US Government and renting a house at 516 Park Avenue in Little Chute, Wisconsin.

Lena died on March 14, 1945 after a short illness at age 58. She had lived in Little Chute for 26 years.

Phillip Cornelius died at 60 years of age on December 15, 1948 and was buried in the Holy Apostles Church Cemetery in Oneida, Wisconsin.

Sampson Cornelius

Sampson Cornelius was born in New York before his family migrated to Wisconsin. There, they lived at West De Pere. On December 20, 1899, six months after completing three years at Hampton Institute, Samson Cornelius arrived at Carlisle for a five-year term of enrollment.

On Washington's birthday in 1900 he attempted to enlist in the Army but was greatly disappointed when he was rejected for "defective vision, which is rare in an Indian." At the end of March, he went on outing to a farm in Wycombe, Pennsylvania and returned to Carlisle in time for the start of the fall term and football season.

The only mention of Sampson Cornelius regarding the Carlisle football team was a comment from Pop Warner that he was a candidate for left halfback. He considered Joel Cornelius for right halfback. The Carlisle backfield was loaded with talent, so getting playing time would

Name:	Sampson Cornelius Jr.	Nickname:	
DOB:	2/19/1878	Height:	5'9½"
Weight:	162 lbs.	Age:	19
Parents:	Wesley Cornelius Sarah Cornelius	Home:	De Pere, WI
Early Schooling:	Hampton Institute		
Later Schooling:	Flandreau Indian School		

have been difficult. A Cornelius got into the Gettysburg and Steelton YMCA games at fullback, but that was probably Joel because he was more experienced. Few substitutes got to play against the tougher opponents. However, games were scheduled for the Second Team or Scrubs. Sampson may have got playing time in those games. Unfortunately, newspapers didn't cover those games in this time period.

At the end of March 1901, he went on outing to a farm at Newtown, Pennsylvania. He ran away and didn't return to Carlisle.

On February 18, 1909, he married Sarah Green, a widow with two daughters, Mamie & Vera, The former Sarah Archiquette worked as head laundress at Flandreau Indian School in South Dakota. She was also a Carlisle alum. It's not clear where he was working at the time. Flandreau would have provided him the best chance of meeting Sarah.

In November 1910, he was working as an asst. engineer at Flandreau, South Dakota with a salary of $600 per year. A serious eye problem forced him to resign and go to Chicago for treatment.

Sampson and Sarah soon had two daughters of their own, Lillian and Iona, born in 1911 and 1913.

In 1915, not satisfied with the quality of education at Flandreau, Wittenberg, and the local public school, Sarah enrolled Mamie and Vera at Carlisle. In 1917, Mamie wanted to marry George May, a football player who was joining the Army. Because Mamie was underage, Superintendent Francis wouldn't give her permission unless her mother agreed. Sarah's cousin told her George had "colored blood" and she withdrew her permission. Apparently, Mamie didn't run off and elope because her mother requested her daughters be allowed to return home in April 1918.

> "I need their help as we put in 1 acre of beans and ½ acre of beans to be picked green for the canning factory....I am all alone on the farm. My husband is working in the paper mill. The men [who normally do this kind of work] are scarce to find."

The war effort created jobs for many and made finding farm and other workers difficult. On July 29th, the school sent Sarah a letter:

"I am sorry to inform you that Vera overstepped our rules the other evening during the time the pupils were having a lawn social. She went to a forbidden part of the grounds with one of the boys and was with him for quite a while. We have had to watch Vera very closely during the whole time she has been at Carlisle, and have never allowed her to go to an outing home after her first summer at Carlisle, and then because we felt we could not trust her with boys."

He sent the sisters home on the train the next day.

Sampson was 40 when he filled out his WWI Draft Registration. He listed his occupation as moving houses and his employer as Henry Kerd. The registrar wrote, "Has lost two fingers," on his card. He surely didn't get drafted at 40 and the war ended two months after he registered.

In April 1919, he was listed among the "True Blue Americans" for subscribing for his allotment of the third liberty loan.

In May, Sarah's brother, Sergeant Wilbert Archiquette, was released from the German prison camp at Rastatt. He returned to his unit, Battery A, 77th Field Artillery. Later that month, Sampson sold a 39-acre parcel to Sylvester Cornelius for $2,500 and bought a 9-acre piece from him for $725.

In 1920, Sampson was working as a carpenter and Sarah as a cook in a restaurant. They, their daughters, and one stepdaughter lived at 903 Elmore Street in Green Bay. Mamie had married Guy Elm, an Oneida who had attended Carlisle. She may have been living with her parents while her husband was in the service.

Sampson died of undisclosed causes on May 14, 1922.

Wallace Denny

Wallace Denny lived at Carlisle Indian School longer than any other student—except his wife, that is. Wallace, 17, and his sister, Elizabeth, 14, arrived at Carlisle on August 12, 1896 in the care of Miss Lamason. They were the children of Josh and Melinda Denny, who appears to have died shortly before their enrollment. Of their older siblings, Wilson was already on his own, Charles may have died, and Louisa may have married. Younger siblings Amos, Mary, and Ida were still at home. Wallace had 50 months of prior schooling and entered at the third grade level. Little else is known about their lives prior to attending Carlisle because all that remains of their student files are two of Wallace's historical record cards. They may have attended a mission school but there is no documentation of that. None of their siblings appear to have attended Carlisle. Elizabeth may have known some English prior to coming because she was chosen to represent her room, Number 1, in

Name:	Wallace Denny		Nickname:	Doctor, Chief
DOB:	11/10/1879		Height:	5'8½"
Weight:	140 lbs.		Age:	17
Parents:	Joshua Denny		Home:	De Pere, WI
	Melinda Denny (deceased)			
Early Schooling:	50 months?			
Later Schooling:				

the December Exhibition. Little is known about Wallace's early education, including the part received at Carlisle. Like other students, he went on outings to work on farms. His first assignments were to Bucks County, Pennsylvania where he worked for various members of the Kirk family on their farms located near Newtown and in Buckingham Township. But he was always back for the start of football season. While at Carlisle, he worked in the Clothing Room.

Wallace Denny was an excellent athlete, very fleet afoot. Unfortunately for him, he arrived at a time when the school was loaded with good athletes, particularly football players. He was on the team but didn't play in games. That changed in 1899 when Pop Warner took the reins as head coach. He enlisted Wallace to be his utility man whose duties consisted of those of an equipment manager, trainer (often called "rubber" at that time) and sometime substitute for an injured player. He quickly became Warner's right hand man but preferred to remain in the background. He didn't shift from competition to a support role in all sports, just football, as he continued to run track in the spring. School papers made no mention of Denny working in a shop. Perhaps learning to be a trainer was his trade. When his enrollment was up in 1901, he returned home. He reenrolled for another five-year term at the beginning of football season and soon started getting some press. From the November 22, 1901 edition of *The Red Man and Helper*:

> "While Mr. Denny, "the rubber man" of the football team, was with the boys at Annapolis last week, he had an experience which caused considerable laughter from the rest of the boys. Mr. Denny becoming very thirsty began to look around in the station for something to satisfy his thirst. On going up to the supposed water-cooler which stood in the corner of the room, he proceeded to fumble around for the spigot, but found to his chagrin that it was not a water tank but a fire extinguisher instead."

As part of the joint Freshman and Sophomore class entertainment in May 1902, Wallace participated in "a laughable dialog" (a skit, one supposes) with Philip Tousey, Phineas Wheelock, and Henry Mitchell. He was a rising Sophomore at that time. In the summer, he and Goliath Bigjim attended the Y. M. C. A. Student Convention at Northfield, a predecessor of Moody Bible Institute located in northwestern Massachusetts. After the rest of the students returned in the fall, he gave a talk on his experiences there to the large boys[3]. In the winter he played on his class's basketball team alongside Wilson Charles, Joel Cornelius, Randolph Hill, and Thomas Gardner. He also joined the Invincible Debating Society and took an active part in their programs.

Wallace Denny as a student

In March 1903, over 50 candidates for the track team competed with each other in the school's first indoor meet. He finished second in the 35-yd dash behind Wilson Charles. Wallace didn't only run track,

---

[3] Carlisle students were grouped by age and physical size in two groups: large and small.

as Coach Warner's assistant, it was his job to help get the track in shape for the season. But that didn't slow him down. In the annual class meet, Denny placed third in the 100-yd dash behind Frank Mt. Pleasant and Wilson Charles. In the 220, he finished a very close second to Mt. Pleasant, so close, in fact, that *The Red Man and Helper* remarked, "Frank Mt. Pleasant and Wallace Denny made the 220 yards dash intensively interesting, so close did they keep together." He joined forces with some of the fastest boys ever to attend Carlisle Indian School to win at the Penn Relays:

> "Wallace Denny was the first runner and he came in ahead by about five yards. Wilson Charles increased the lead materially, and James Johnson and Frank Mt. Pleasant then 'took it easy' and finished about twenty yards ahead of their opponents. Besides winning a banner for the school the boys each won a gold watch with the names of the contesting colleges engraved on the back.

Wallace Denny with sweatbox

"The team could have made much better time if it had been necessary to exert themselves in order to win."

Wallace Denny spent the summer at Carlisle and received praise for filling in for a school employee, Disciplinarian Thompson, who was also in charge of the large boys. In the fall, it was reported, "Wallace Denny is again at his old work as 'Doctor' of the football squad." Doctor Denny continued his work throughout the season and accompanied the team on its postseason trip to play football games in Salt Lake City, San Francisco, and Los Angeles.

In the spring of 1904, Denny again donned his track togs. In the annual class meet, he finished third in the 100-yd dash and 220-yd dash. Against other schools, he placed second in the meet with Bucknell and received kudos for his teamwork against Penn State:

> "Although he did not score any points, much of the success of the team is due to Wallace Denny. Besides taking good care of the boys he went in the quarter-mile run and set such a hot pace that, in trying to prevent him from getting the lead the State College man so exhausted himself that Mt. Pleasant easily passed him in the home stretch, and won in a jog. Denny could have probably scored points in the 220-yd dash but through an oversight or error of judgment was not put in that event."

That spring, Wallace gained a stepmother. His widowed father married Isabel Cornelius, Oneida, a Carlisle graduate and teacher of both white and Indian children, on Easter Sunday. In the years following the union, his father and 26-year younger bride gave him two half-siblings, Josh Jr. and Grace. Wallace was surely unable to attend the wedding due to distance and school obligations.

Wallace's two-month outing that year was spent with Mrs. Jennie Cook, a widow who ran a boarding house in Chautauqua, New York. It's fair to assume he assisted her in operating during the resort season and he attended some lectures in his spare time.

Pop Warner left Carlisle before the start of the 1904 football season but Denny retained his position as utility man. Among his tasks for home games, of which there were quite a few, was the lining off of the field. After the Harvard game, the *Boston Herald* reported, "[Umpire] Bill Edwards was kept busy watching the Indian medicine man. There was a strong suspicion that the Indian was carrying messages from the side lines." Carl Flanders, the former star center at Yale, who later assisted at Carlisle, shed some light on the possibility that Denny was in fact carrying in plays along with water:

> "Wallace Denny and Bemus Pierce got up a code of signals, using an Indian word which designated a single play. Among the Indian words which designated these signals were Water-bucket, Watehnee, Coocoohee. I never could find out what it all meant, and following the Indian team by this code of signals was a task which was too much for me."

That November, the school had its first ever political meeting, an event that mimicked a political party convention. The band played as students marched in and took their seats. The room was decorated with banners supporting the different candidates. Several people spoke, supporting this or that candidate or party, including Wallace Denny:

> "Another Republican from Wisconsin, who was introduced as a great traveler, through which privilege he had enjoyed rare opportunities of feeling the political pulse of the country, then came to the front mid cheers and. yells. It was our popular Wallace Denny, class '06, and he surprised the audience by his clear-cut logic and quiet eloquence. His speech was pronounced by all as the best of the evening, in the surprises it held for the audience. Wallace has had to combat an impediment in his speech, and has labored under the greatest difficulties to pronounce correctly. His address last Monday evening showed how well he has mastered all, and on inquiry,

his friends learned he has been drilling incessantly in school exercises, having come out conqueror.

"Cool-headed and strong were his arguments in favor of the present administration of public affairs. He showed how Roosevelt had come in closer touch with the people than had any other president. The attacks that had been made upon Roosevelt, every president had suffered.

"It was not an uncommon thing for the people to criticize the executive officer of our Government.

"Denny took his seat amid storms of applause and the tension of the audience was relaxed by singing 'America.'"

In December, while participating in the student government, Representative Denny of the Junior Class proposed a bill requiring compulsory education for students from 11 to 14 years of age. His bill failed to pass.

As the calendar turned to 1905, Wallace continued his participation with the Invincibles, with a select reading, possibly as part of his speech therapy. At the Inter-Society Debate in March, he, Albert Exendine and Antonio Rodriquez represent the Invincibles as they defeated the Standards' position as argued by Chauncey Charles, Nicholas Pena, and James Parsons. The question the Indians debated was: "That legislation to further restrict and better control immigration into the United States should be enacted." Which side he took was not reported. About a decade later, a student, Lewis Braun, testified that the boys disrespected Denny and, probably confusing a speech impediment with poor knowledge of the language, described his speech as broken English. The transcript of Denny's testimony at the 1914 Joint Congressional Inquiry reflected something other than broken English. In the spring, Wallace Denny went out for track again, both on the varsity squad and for his class, the Seniors, team for which he was elected captain. *The Arrow* reported he would be competing in the 100-yd dash, 220-yd dash, and 440-yd dash. He placed third in the 100-yd dash and first in the 440 in the annual Inter-Class Contest, with his points helping the Senior Class to win the meet. Later, he placed second in the 220 in the dual meet with Penn State. At the end of the spring term, he left for Chautauqua where he again spent the summer. That summer, he also took a course on massage, a subject with which he was already experienced. At the beginning of football season, *The Arrow* reported, "'Dr.' Denny will again have charge of the 'rubbers.' Better results than ever are expected from him because of his special studies this summer." Although listed on the roster as a player, he didn't play much if at all; his role was ministering to the injured.

Wallace continued his participation with the Invincibles who elected him vice-president. He began to be more involved in social events that year. In February 1906, he stood up for Charles Dillon as a groomsman in his wedding to Rosa La Forge. The next month he was among a group of Episcopalian students invited to attend a party hosted

Wallace Denny visiting his family in Wisconsin

by Mrs. Ege at Metzger Institute, a woman's college located in Carlisle. They played Clap In and Clap Out, Feather, and "...some games that taxed the mental powers...." After having refreshments, participants danced the Virginia Reel to the tune pounded out by Mrs. Ege on the piano. Also attending were Marian Powlas, Elizabeth Baird, Dora LaBelle, Blanche Lay, Electa Metoxen, Adaline Kingsley, Thomas Eagleman, Thomas Saul, Abram Hill, Ignatius Ironroad, William Jones, Miss Gedney, and Miss Nellie Robertson.

Wallace Denny graduated as a member of the Class of 1906 in late March. The Commencement edition of *The Arrow* included an article titled "Farming" he wrote. In that piece, he advised Indian youth of the day to learn about farming because they were landowners and, while they may never farm the land themselves, may lease the land to others to do the actual work. He went on to discuss various aspects of farming they would need to know something about.

After graduation, at about 28 years of age, he became Mr. Denny, a member of the staff of Carlisle Indian School. His duties were not much different than they had been as a senior student. He was assistant disciplinarian in charge of the small boys and was the utility man for the Athletic Association. One of his first tasks was to put the track in shape for the season that was just starting. After serving as a groomsman for Wilson Charles in his wedding to Elizabeth Knudsen, he headed west to Wisconsin for vacation. Little was heard of him after his vacation until January 1907 at the annual Athletic Banquet at which he was reunited with his old mentor, Pop Warner, who had just returned as Carlisle Athletic Director. This time Wallace had a speaking part. That was probably due to his becoming an employee of the school and of the Athletic Association. His "...humorous little dissertation gave us the 'Bright Side of Indian Football.'" As an acknowledgement of his position on the staff of the school, he served as starter and timer for the annual cross country race held during Commencement Week during the first week of April that year.

On June 12, 1907, a Wednesday, Wallace Denny married Nellie V. Robertson in the Teachers' Parlor in a simple but beautiful setting. The ceremony was conducted under a canopy of daisies, the flower most prominent in the decorations. Anna Goueutuey, Pueblo, a teacher at the school was maid of honor. Hastings M. Robertson, cousin of the bride and graduate of Dickinson School of Law class of '07, was best man. Miss Ella G. Hill played the piano. The bride wore a white gown and carried a bouquet of roses. Wallace was dressed in conventional black. Rev. McMillan of the Episcopal Church in Carlisle performed the ceremony. Nellie's boss, Miss Anne Ely, head of the outing system and namesake of present-day Ely Hall on Carlisle Barracks, gave the bride away. After the reception, Mr. and Mrs. Denny honeymooned in New York City and at New Jersey resorts.

Nellie V. Robertson

Nellie V. Robertson

On November 6, 1880, barely a year after Carlisle Indian School first opened, Nellie V. Robertson, 9, arrived from the Sisseton Agency dressed like any other American schoolgirl of the day. Nellie, the daughter of a white man, Angus Robertson, and an unknown deceased Sioux woman, enrolled for a three-year term. She had less than a year of prior schooling and knew little English. The 1887 census, the earliest one found listing her, included an older sister, Etta, and a younger brother, Wilder. Her remaining school records do not include anything about her father except his name, he lived in Brown's Valley, and her mother was dead. She may have had older siblings who were living on their own at that time but that is not known.

Nellie must have had learned something in the little bit of schooling she had before arriving at Carlisle because, just eight months later, she wrote a piece that was published in *The School News,* "Nellie Robertson's thoughts on Moses in the Bulrushes." While clearly written by a child, the writing reflects a better command of English than eight month's exposure would suggest. In January 1882, she wrote a short letter to Capt. Pratt to apologize for speaking an Indian word. Alice

Wynn spoke to her in Sioux and she reflexively started to respond in her mother tongue. Just one word got out before she stopped herself but she felt so badly about the incident that she couldn't finish her supper and cried. She wrote, "I tried very hard to speak only English." That month she also wrote her father to tell him all about her Christmas and the gifts she received. She wished Annie, Wilder, and Etta well. Perhaps Annie was an older sister who was married or living on her own. She also told him how hard she was trying to excel in school.

Nellie spent three weeks that summer and the last half of 1883 on outings, first in Philadelphia then in Willow Grove. She returned home in June of 1884, a year after her three-year term was up. It isn't known what she did for the next three years, but on August 12, 1887 she returned for a five-year enrollment.

Due to being older and an excellent student, Nellie Robertson's name more frequently adorned the pages of the school newspaper, which was then called *The Indian Helper*. She became active in the girls' literary society, often serving as an officer and was placed in charge of C Company. When she was a senior, Nellie started studying with the Normal Department. She also sang alto in the school choir. In January 1890, as part of a school exhibition, Nellie played a piano duet with Miss Moore, a faculty member, to open the exercises. Nellie also served as President of "Whatsoever Circle," which was previously known as The King's Daughter's Society.

On April 14, 1890 Nellie V. Robertson graduated from Carlisle Indian School. She began her valedictory address as follows:

> "Dear Friends, allow me to take you for a moment out on an Indian reservation as it is to-day. It is a place from which almost all signs of civilization and education are excluded, where broad acres of land lie uncultivated; a prison as it were, where our people, the prisoners waste their lives away in idleness, while their white brothers feed and clothe them. The only homes they know are miserable and comfortless log huts or tepees. Their amusements are of the wildest sorts.

"They delight in sun-dances and other barbarous doings where they can torture themselves. Their travelling is done by walking or on horseback. They are an ignorant and uneducated people. True many of the young Indians are being educated at schools, but what will they ever do? Will they ever be the means of bringing the Indians to live and so as the white men?"

She then predicted what her classmates will have accomplished thirty years after graduation. All were depicted as functioning well in the white man's world. Some were even prospering abroad. She was accurate about one of them: Dennison Wheelock did become a successful band leader and, later, a lawyer. More research is needed to determine how accurately she predicted the future overall. Nellie had fully absorbed the lesson Superintendent Pratt intended her to internalize. In a later issue, her fantasy piece, "A Trip to the Moon," describe a world created in her imagination that would not be unfamiliar to fans of 1950s science fiction movies. After graduation, she and Eva Johnson were rewarded with a pleasant country home for the summer of 1890. They stayed with E. Austin in Oak Lane, Pennsylvania until mid-September at which time she returned home to her family.

A month later, *The Indian Helper* announced that she and her sister, Etta, were returning to Carlisle. Apparently, Etta had previously attended the school, but few of her records survived. They arrived in late-October and Nellie matriculated at Metzger Institute, a College for Young Ladies, in Carlisle. Its close proximity made it possible for her to continue her participation in extra-curricular activities at the Indian School. She continued to do well in her studies and led the white girls in three of her classes. Etta followed in her sister's footsteps and led her classmates in room Number 12 but returned home in July 1891 after graduating. Less than two years after that, she married Solomon Renville, the son of a native preacher. Etta died in 1894.

Nellie filled in as assistant matron over the summer to cover vacations. In September, Nellie and Rosa Bourassa returned to their studies at Metzer Institute. Still participating in Indian School activities, she played another piano duet with Miss Moore at a school exhibition in

October. She also played for the Christmas Eve festivities in the girls' quarters. In the spring, Nellie and some other girls gathered arbutus at Hunter's Run. One assumes she graduated from Metzger that spring because, after spending her summer in Oak Lawn with E. Austin again, she enrolled at West Chester Normal School in West Chester, Pennsylvania.

Except for breaks in the school year, Nellie stayed in West Chester. She spent her 1893 spring break and summer vacation at Carlisle. In the summer, she filled in as an assistant in the school's hospital. She continued her studies at the normal school until the end of January 1894, at which time she returned home for unspecified reasons and stayed there. Perhaps she was needed to help out with Etta who died that year. No quitter, Nellie returned to West Chester in November 1894 to complete her studies. While at West Chester, Principal Dr. George Phillips said she won the love and respect of them all. She graduated in June 1896. Her article, "Sensitiveness to Sound in English Poets," was published in the school's literary journal, *The Amulet*. It was reprinted in the May-June issue of *The Red Man*.

After graduation, Nellie helped with clerical work in the Carlisle School office for a bit before heading out to the Sisseton Agency to recruit students. She returned with seven pupils. In September, Miss Robertson began her teaching career in room Number 7. In November, she gave a talk in front of the whole school on "Helen Keller as a Harvard student." Keller did not attend Harvard, of course, because women were not admitted in her day. She did attend and graduated from Radcliff College cum laude years after Nellie gave this talk. One wonders what the point of her talk was. Could it have had to do with women not being allowed into Harvard or could it have been about the ability of a severely handicapped person to be able to do work at the level required to meet Harvard's standards? Her next talk was on "The World's Advance during Queen Victoria's Reign." She spent the summer of 1897 at Chautauqua as she would many succeeding summers. But not all. In 1899, she visited her family and friends in South Dakota and returned with six girls and one boy. Then she spent some time at the New Jersey Shore.

After four years of teaching, Nellie shifted to doing clerical work under Anne Ely in the Outing Office at a salary of $660 per year. In addition, she would hold down the fort during Miss Ely's absences. At the celebration of the school's twenty-second anniversary in October 1901, Colonel Pratt said, "I think we ought to hear from a student from among the first who came to us." After several people called out her name, Pratt said, "Miss Robertson, will you please say a word?" She responded:

> "I feel that I can add but little to the commendable things that have been heard here to-night, so shall not try, but simply stand so you can see an example of one brought from barbarian into civilization by Carlisle."

Always a sociable person, Nellie acquired a ping pong set in March 1902 and attracted many guests. That summer, she broke with her traditions and summered at Beaver Falls, Minnesota. However, she visited friends and relatives in South Dakota before arriving there. Much work greeted her on her return as early September was her busy season. She, Anne Ely, and Emma Skye had to make the ticket arrangements for 202 boys and 144 girls to return from summer outings. On November 6, she was the guest of honor at a surprise party to celebrate the twenty-second anniversary of her arrival at the school. She was presented with a dozen fruit knives to commemorate the event.

Nellie continued to work in the Outing Office and to take her vacations at Chautauqua or visit South Dakota. Suddenly, the rhythm of her life changed.

Wallace and Nellie Denny

After the Dennys returned from their honeymoon, they took up residence at Carlisle Barracks. He continued his work as Assistant Disciplinarian and she as the Head Clerk in the Outing Office. He didn't give up sports just because he was married. Shortly after their return, he played catcher for the Big Chiefs in a game against the Young Chiefs. Jim Thorpe pitched for the Big Chiefs and Wallace handled his throws with perfection. William Garlow pitched for the Young Chiefs. The seven-inning game ended in a 5-5 tie.

In the fall, Wallace continued his role as trainer for the football team. He even received a little coverage from the school newspaper:

> "During the Penn'sy game Mr. Denny, the great Indian trainer, was again in his form of younger days by always following the ball. His brilliant 45-yd. run on the side line was a spectacle."

After their marriage, coverage of their activities became less frequent, but was sufficient to gain an idea of what the Dennys were doing. For example, rather than vacationing separately, they traveled together to see her friends and family in South Dakota, likely stopping off in Wisconsin to spend some time with his. Their working lives changed little at first, other than living together in the small boys quarters. Wallace kept active supporting the athletic programs and honing his tennis game.

As far as income was concerned, the Dennys were in an enviable position. In December 1909, Nellie's salary was increased to $900 a year. When she became Outing Manager in 1911, her salary increased to $1,000. Add to that Wallace's salary as Assistant Disciplinarian and the amount paid to him by the Athletic Association for his work as trainer and you have a tidy sum. Wallace and Nellie were used as success stories in Carlisle publications. In 1910, Wallace and Nellie were tasked to travel about the U. S. to the various Indian Agencies to interview former Carlisle students and report on their then present conditions. By that time, Wallace's job title had changed to Assistant Commander of Cadets. It brought with it an increase from $720 to $750 per year and in 1911 to $800. The school's administration was surely happy with their report:

> "Their report is very pleasing as they find that while they often pick up the-shawl and blanket, they are good housekeepers, good cooks and have many of the lessons taught them in the school, and are making good use of. Mrs. Pedrick aided them in locating the old students and showing them the difference in the Indians

who have never attended school and the ones who have graduated."

Wallace and Nellie Denny became institutions at the school after Superintendent Pratt left. Soon, they had more institutional knowledge than other faculty members. Occasionally, articles were written about one or the other of them in school publications. In April 1912, Iva Miller described room Number 14, the Seniors' home room as being haunted. She described it as being

> "...full of sweet memories of classes that have gone forth ready to begin their life battle. Strong and noble characters have left the impress of their personality upon this spot, so that he who understands and realizes the significance of this room, feels that it is a blessed thing to have- the privilege of assembling here. It is impossible to recall the names of those who have created the 'atmosphere' of this room, but we all think at once of two names which stand out from the rest: Mrs. N. R. Denny and Charles Dagenette, whose strong personalities seem always with us. They are loved by all with whom they come in contact and are looked up to by all Indians who know them."

That spring, the Dennys set up housekeeping in a cottage next to the athletic quarters and Wallace spent his summer there. No mention was made of how Nellie spent her time but an item that appeared in the September 20, 1912 edition of *The Carlisle Arrow* suggested something:

Congratulations to Mr. and Mrs. Denny

"A dear little son arrived at the home of Mr. and Mrs. Wallace Denny on the evening of the 12th. His name is Wallace Robertson Denny. Everyone on the Campus extends a loving greeting to Wallace, Junior, and congratulations to his parents in the happy event of his coming."

Nellie was well past 40 at the time and probably had abandoned hope of ever having a child, especially after five years of marriage. So, little Robertson, as he was called by many, was truly an unexpected bundle of joy for his parents. The school newspaper reported the details of his life. One can only imagine how the students doted on this toddler. He was baptized in March 1913 at St. John's Episcopal Church with Rev. Alexander McMillan officiating. Nellie's cousins Elsie Robertson and Robert Weatherstone sponsored him. In October, the Dennys moved back into their old apartment on the first floor at the end of the Small Boys Quarters. The apartment had been improved in their absence and had been given a new coat of paint. It had likely proved a necessity for Wallace to be living closer to his young charges. At 15 months, Little Robertson joined the Invincible Debating Society by placing his thumb print beside his written name. Two months later, he was walking. With his newfound mobility he patrolled the campus when he wanted. At 26 months, he visited the stables daily. Two weeks later, he added the laundry to his daily rounds. In February 1915, when he was two and a half, Robert Broker and Ben Swallow made a pony cart for Wallace. In May, he had a picture taken of his pony. Wallace's pony, Steiner Girl, won a blue ribbon at the Carlisle Fair in October. It is likely that both the pony and the cart were intended for Little Robertson. The doting father even had a cavalry uniform tailored for the boy. Winsome, Little Robertson's second pony, arrived in March 1918. The Shetland ponies became fixtures around campus and in town as well when they pulled a wagon decorated with flags and bunting in the Liberty Loan parade.

The Dennys continued their work at the school. Wallace's responsibilities increased over time while Nellie took a couple of years off during Little Robertson's infancy. She then returned to her former position as head of the Outing Program. When the 1914 Joint Congressional Inquiry rocked the campus, both Dennys were interviewed, even though Nellie wasn't an employee at the time. She testified that the school didn't provide students on outing with adequate shoes, students complained about a shortage of bread, and food is not always properly cooked in the school's dining hall. She also testified about discord between Superintendent Friedman and several teachers and either the superintendent or the disgruntled teachers must leave to eliminate the problem.

Wallace Denny testified that discipline problems began when Major Mercer as superintendent allowed two or three sociables a week at which students were allowed to dance. When Moses Friedman reduced the number to one reception and one sociable a month, students turned against him. He also testified that schoolwork became more difficult under Friedman. He also told the committee how he had prompted an investigation into the lack of bread for students. As it turned out, the bakery turned out plenty of good quality bread but the Quartermaster would only allow so much to be given to students, citing regulations that limit how much he could give them. Denny was interrogated about a couple of incidents in which he was accused of punching some students. In one case, the student punched him first when he wasn't looking. The other incident involved a tough who came straight to Carlisle from jail. When asked about problems with students drinking, he pointed out that the drinkers arrived at the school with the habit and they weren't becoming drinkers there. He considered drinking to be a major problem.

The commission recommended that Wallace Denny be reprimanded for punching a student. Wallace continued in his position. After the inquiry, it appears he did more things to endear himself to students than he had done before. Treats included picnics in parks, watermelons, use of the kitchen, and camping trips. One night after feasting on watermelons, the small boys cheered Denny loudly as they marched into their quarters: "Watermelon, Denny! Watermelon, Denny! Rah, rah, rah!"

Wallace and Nellie became active in the Society of American Indians. Part of their involvement was attending conferences around the country. Nellie became very active in the Alumni Association and returned to work as head of the Outing Department. Whenever Gen. Pratt would visit, Nellie and Wallace would meet and dine with him as well as stand with him in receiving lines. In March 1918, Nellie had the great honor of making the presentation of a gift from Pratt to the Susan

Longstreth[4] Literary Society at his request. Pratt had 100 letters from Susan Longstreth to him bound in the form of a book. This book was to remain in the hands of the Society and members were to be read from it periodically.

Wallace continued to be involved in school athletics, particularly in track, which he coached after Pop Warner left in 1915. He continued to improve his tennis game and in 1916 won the tennis championship of Carlisle and vicinity by beating a number of players from Dickinson College and Conway Hall. He won the trophy by defeating the 1915 champion, Robert E. Woodward. It appears that Wallace didn't serve as trainer for the football team after Warner left because, in later years, he recalled working with Warner in Pittsburgh. Warner left Carlisle in 1915 to coach Pitt and stayed there through the 1923 season. Denny wasn't needed at Carlisle in 1915 because Head Coach Victor Kelley brought Uncle Charlie Moran up from Texas A&M with him. Carlisle's football program was a shambles the last two years it competed, 1916 and 1917. Denny probably didn't think Carlisle would need him when the 1916 season started without a schedule of games in place.

Nellie was mired in a protracted communication with the Bureau of Indian Affairs over her land in 1916, 1917, and 1918. Eventually, she was awarded her share of the Sisseton-Wahpeton Tribal Fund, the patent for her land, as well as a citizenship pin and bag because she became a citizen when she accepted her allotment. At a particularly frustrating point in the process, Superintendent John Francis wrote the superintendent of the Sisseton Indian Agency:

> "In response you are advised that Mrs. Denny is an employee at this school, having charge of the Outing work. She has received a patent for all her property and is just as capable as you or me in taking care of it, in fact Mr. and Mrs. Denny have accumulated quite a bit of property themselves. I dislike even to suggest to her that she should have this money to her credit and supervise."

---

[4] Quakers Susan Longstreth & her sister Mary Anna, retired from operating a school for girls in Philadelphia, were ardent supporters of Carlisle Indian School.

Wallace Denny, Wallace Robertson Denny & Nellie Robertson Denny

Apparently, the Dennys were doing quite well financially and owned a significant amount of real estate. Later evidence of this was the 1930 census that valued their home in San Jose, California at $5,000.

Shortly after the U. S. entered WWI, former Superintendent Oscar Lipps wrote Nellie regarding the frenzy of boys enlisting in the armed forces:

> "If the war fever strikes Carlisle I am afraid it will greatly interfere with your outing. I should put it up to the boys that they can show their patriotism by taking up the hoe just as fully as by taking up a gun. We are going to need food, and Mr. Sells thinks the Carlisle boys can perform a distinct service for their country by going out on farms and helping to raise food supplies. I think so, too."

Carlisle Indian School supported the war effort in many ways including donating money, making bandages and garments for the Red Cross, and marching in parades to raise support and funds for the war. Although Carlisle Indian School closed suddenly on September 1, 1918–a 9-game football schedule was already in place–Wallace and Nellie Denny stayed on.

Carlisle Barracks was returned to the Army for use as a hospital in which soldiers wounded in France were treated. Wallace served as athletic director for the installation. What Nellie did at this time isn't clear. Because of their longevity with the Indian School and that they remained at the post after its conversion to a military hospital, Wallace and Nellie were in a unique position to dispose of school artifacts. A 1934 letter from the Dennys to Samuel M. Goodyear of Carlisle discussed how various items were disposed of when the school closed. C. V. Peel of the Indian Bureau authorized them to handle the disposal of the property. Government property, including records, was sent to Washington; school publications were given to General Pratt, Bosler Memorial Library in Carlisle, and the State Library in Harrisburg as were some other materials later, in 1922. Things like pictures and trophies paid for with Athletic Fund monies were retained by the Dennys. Later, when the Hamilton Library (part of Cumberland County Historical Society) established a Carlisle Indian School room, the Dennys recommended that the State Library transfer its holdings to the newly formed room.

The Dennys stayed in Carlisle until April 1922 when it was announced that Wallace had taken a job as athletic trainer at Stanford University. Warner had accepted the coaching job but would not move to Pala Alto until after the 1923 season because he was compelled to honor the terms of his contract with Pitt. He sent two assistants ahead to run the Stanford team and teach his system to them. Wallace Denny was part of his coaching team. Andy Kerr, Tiny Thornhill, and Wallace Denny coached the Cardinals until Warner was free of his entanglement with Pittsburgh. Wallace's quiet competence quickly caught *Oakland Tribune* reporter Doug Montell's eye:

> "The quietest, most efficient, and shyest man on Stanford field these days is Wallace Denny, former Carlisle Indian and present Stanford trainer. Denny likes a camera like a cat likes water, claiming that his place is not in the front line before the camera but behind the scenes turning out athletes in the pink of condition. Yet Denny never misses a moment of practice and so thoroughly does he know the ins and outs of football that

were Kerr and Thornnill ever called away Denny could conduct practice from where they had left off without a hitch."

Almost nine years later, in April 1931, still at Stanford, Denny drew the attention of Frank Wilton who wrote about him in *The San Mateo Times and Daily News Leader*.

> "'I fix you up, buddy!' is the pet expression of Wallace Denny, the Stanford athletic trainer. With the fixing up expression as his introduction, Denny proceeds to do a little rubbing of the sore muscle and a lot of talking about how he used to do it when he was a young man."

Wallace Robertson Denny's doting father wanted him to attend Stanford. Wilton wrote, "My boy is a fine boy. He goes to San Jose State Teachers' College now. I think he will come to Stanford soon and be under 'Pop'." Wallace also told the reporter about his old teammate: "Jim Thorpe was a great Indian. You know, he was a mean player. He was a great athlete—he liked to hit you hard."

After the end of the 1932 season, Pop Warner announced he was leaving Stanford to take the head coaching job at Temple. Wallace Denny joined him in Philadelphia. Nellie died on May 1, 1935 at 64 years of age. Wallace, being younger than his late wife, continued working after her death. In 1936, he remarried to Rosa Bourassa LaFlesche, a widowed former Carlisle student and Nelie's co-worker at the school.

Al Worden of *The Ogden Standard-Examiner* interviewed Denny in 1936 and got an interesting quote: "Football is just about perfect these days. I've seen hundreds of games since the late 90s and have watched the game improve tremendously. And say, the attendance is certainly ahead of what it was in the long, long ago."

In 1937, at almost 60, Wallace won the campus tennis championship by beating student Meyer Perchonock, Temple's best varsity player, in straight sets. Denny claimed not to have lost a match in 15 years. He continued working at Temple through the 1938 season after which Pop Warner left. He was replaced by former Temple track and gymnastics star Frank Wiechic but he wasn't ready to retire yet and neither was Pop.

They found something to do close to their homes in Palo Alto and Santa Clara, respectively. Warner accepted the position as advisory coach at San Jose State Teachers' College and Wallace Denny took his familiar place alongside him for the start of the 1939 season. AP Feature Service Writer Sam Jackson caught up with "Chief" Denny, as the players called him, in San Jose late that year when his team was the highest-scoring outfit in the country. Jackson wrote,

> "When you overcome the Chief's natural reticence, he'll take you into the field house and show you the pads and appliances he's concocted to protect various injuries. They're secrets between the trainer and Pop, he says. No other handler knows these exact tricks. Like many trainers, Denny works his psychology hard. He constantly watches the boys on the field, knows how to handle each one to get the most out of him. Problems that a player is backward about laying before the coach are often threshed out with the trainer."

Jackson even got Denny to say a few things on the record:

> "Football is harder today than it used to be. The old timers like to think their game was tough, but it wasn't as tough as the open game. Tackling is more deadly. You really need to protect a man more. I don't see any great difference in the physical setup of boys now and forty years ago, but the players today take better care of themselves. I certainly like to win. I used to like to win even if the boys were hurt, but now I protect the boys."

Warner coached and Denny nursed his players one more year. At 1940 season's end, they both retired. Wallace was still in good physical condition and boasted he had never smoked, drank, or chewed. Sam Jackson recalled him saying about Warner, "We've been everywhere else together. When the time comes I guess we'll meet in the Happy

Hunting Ground." Pop Warner died in 1954. Denny died the next year at about 77 years of age after a long illness.

Wallace Denny with tennis racquet

Benjamin Doxtator

Until 1901 he was carried on tribal rolls as Berry (Doxtator) Jourdan. At Carlisle he was called Benjamin Doxtator. His wife was carried on the rolls as Elizabeth Jourdan until 1901. Here, we will refer to him as Benjamin Doxtator, the name he used most of his adult life.

Ben arrived at Carlisle on August 16, 1889 to start a five-year enrollment. He spent his summers, and sometimes more, on outings at farms. He returned from a farm in September 1893 unaware of what was about to happen. In October, Superintendent Pratt rescinded his order against playing football with other schools and allowed a Carlisle team to be formed. Ben played an important position, center, on Carlisle's first team. The short season put together hastily after Pratt made his decision only scheduled three games. After that Ben was back to his usual routine. When his 1894 summer outing ended, his term of enrollment was over, so he returned home.

Name: Benjamin Doxtator	Nickname: Ben
DOB: 12/20/1873	Height: Tall
Weight: 136 lbs.	Age: 16
Parents: George Doxtator Mary Ann Doxtator	Home: De Pere, WI
Early Schooling: Unknown	
Later Schooling: None	

Ben married Elizabeth Smith circa 1895. In 1910 he wrote that they spent nine months at Flandreau Indian School in South Dakota, she as a laundress and he as a farmer. It isn't clear if they met there or if he took her there after getting married. He received little notice in the press throughout his life as he farmed his land. The 1900 Federal Census appeared to have corrected his name after the fact but it did indicate that he owned his own farm. It also listed a son Paul Jr., age 5. Paul wasn't listed on later tribal rolls, so he must have died. In 1902 they had an adopted son.

Ben and Elizabeth led lives out of the limelight working their farm and raising children. Over the next three decades they shared their home with at least ten children, none of whom were their own.

Benjamin Doxtator died on June 29, 1931 at age 57 following an operation. His obituary stated:

> "He was one of the most prosperous Indian farmers on the reservation. He is survived by his wife and ten adopted children, principally orphans whom the couple raised from an early age. Their names are Robertson Jacobs, Sam Smith, James Hill, Daisy Smith, Isabel Smith, Luella John, Lester, Carrie, Estella, and Stephen Jacobs. James Hill, who served in the Navy for seven years, is now home taking charge of the Doxtator farm."

David George

David George arrived at Carlisle on August 25, 1907 at age 12 for a five-year enrollment and was placed in the 3rd Grade. His father was dead and his mother had tuberculosis. His home was on the Onondaga Nation located south of Syracuse, New York. However, he was on Oneida tribal rolls because his parents were Oneida who hadn't relocated to Wisconsin.

David spent the half of his day he wasn't in academic classes learning to be a house painter. His name appeared on the January Merit Roll as the 3rd Grade student with the best average, 9.5. He was tied with Thomas Greene at 9.4 on the Final Merit Roll for the 1907-08 school year. At school's end, he went on two outings, the first in April for an indeterminate time, the second for an entire year beginning in August. Both were farms most likely. He spent the entire 1908-09 and 1909-10

Name:	David Lewis George	Nickname:	
DOB:	6/18/1895	Height:	5'9"
Weight:	161 lbs.	Age:	17
Parents:	Peter George Mary Powless Jacobs	Home:	Syracuse, NY
Early Schooling:	Onondaga Nation School possibly		
Later Schooling:	Auto repair, operation, & sales		

school years at Carlisle. In January 1910 his painting ability evaluation by his school instructor was only Fair although his conduct was Good.

In May 1910, George went on outing to Wormleysburg, a town east of Carlisle in Cumberland County, Pennsylvania. There, he worked with Samuel S. Bear, an independent painter and decorator. A June edition of *The Carlisle Arrow* commented: "David George is one of our weekly visitors. He appears quite contented with his [outing] home, which is near by." Could he have had a girlfriend at Carlisle? He spent the entire summer there. His ability was rated as Very Good for that period.

David spent the entire 1910-11 school year at Carlisle, progressing from 6th grade to 7th by the end of the year. His school instructor only rated his ability as Good. He spent the summer on outing in Wormleysburg again, this time in chunks ranging from two weeks to a month at a time.

In October, he worked on a job west of Carlisle at Greason for two and a half weeks. Perhaps he was painting a barn. In the annual Handicap Track Meet in the spring, he came in 2nd in the high jump behind H. Smith. Jim Thorpe didn't place. At the end of the term he left for his home near Syracuse, his enrollment completed.

David returned on September 29, 1912 to start a second enrollment. This time for three years. On October 12, he got into the Third Team's game at fullback against Harrisburg's Technical High School. This is the only documentation of David George playing on the Carlisle varsity. However, Second Team and Third Team games received infrequent and spotty coverage. Chances are David played on his shop's intramural team some years before trying out for the varsity.

David joined the Standard Debating Society that year and participated in its activities. He remained on campus until June 1913, when he went out on outing to Columbia, Pennsylvania to work for Reinard & Henry until October, likely painting. He spoke about the history of Thanksgiving at the Thanksgiving program in the evening after the feast. In March, his mother wrote the Superintendent requesting that David be allowed to come home for the summer because her husband wouldn't return from Europe until the fall. David came home but didn't return to Carlisle in the fall.

The superintendent forwarded to him the letter from the Commissioner of Indian Affairs awarding him third prize in the essay-writing contest that was conducted through the Indian School Service. He also enclosed the emblem that represented the prize.

He toyed with going to a business school but he couldn't afford the fifty-dollar tuition. He settled on a technical school that covered repairing, operating, and selling automobiles.

The 1915 New York State Census listed him as the husband of the head of the household, Nilia George, an Onondaga approximately his age. The automobile training may not have worked out as he was working as a painter at the time. Listing him as her husband may have been a ruse.

When he registered for the WWI draft in 1917, he was working as a fireman on the New York Central Railroad and was married to Helen Alice George. In 1920, he was still working as a fireman on the railroad, married to Helen George, and had two sons. The Federal Census listed all four of them initially as red but were changed to white. The tribal rolls only listed him, not his wife or children.

The 1930 census had him living with his uncle War Eagle and aunt Louise Powless and working as a mason. His May 21, 1930 New York Marriage License listed Neosta Powless, age 24, an Oneida nurse originally from Wisconsin as his bride. The license said neither had a former spouse. It appears that David surely did have a former spouse but New York law didn't allow divorced people to remarry. The Marriage Certificate showed that the wedding took place the same day.

His August 9, 1935 Pennsylvania Application for Marriage License again stated that he had no previous marriages. His bride was Marjorie A. La Lone, a 31-year-old beautician residing in Syracuse. The reason for marrying in Susquehanna County, Pennsylvania may have been a means to get around New York laws against remarrying.

The 1940 Federal Census had him living at 109 Beacon Street in Syracuse with his unnamed wife and working as a machinist at Coeraldevin Factory.

His WWII Draft Registration Card had him married to an unnamed person, living at 234 Tallman Street in Syracuse, and working at New Process Gear Corporation.

Marjorie L. George was listed as divorced, living at 147 Chester Street in Syracuse, and working as a licensed practical nurse on the 1950 Federal Census. A David George died in 1958 in Onondaga County, New York. However, t is possible this was a different David George.

Levi E. Hill/Hillman

Unsurprisingly, the school recorded his tribe as Onondaga instead of Oneida and often referred to him as Hillman rather than Hill. It's understandable how they got the tribe wrong because he lived in the Onondaga Nation, but where did Hillman come from?

Both his parents were living then. Levi was placed in 6th grade due to having previously attended Thomas Indian School, aka Thomas Asylum of Orphan and Destitute Indian Children, where he also studied carpentry two years. In 1906, he switched to masonry.

The first thing noted on his record after arriving was two months later in April 1904 when he and two other boys ran away for six days. Not known is if they returned on their own volition or why they ran away. His early outings were doing farm work, something he had

Name:	Levi E. Hill/Hillman	Nickname:	
DOB:	3/15/1887	Height:	5'½"
Weight:	145 lbs.	Age:	17
Parents:	William Hill/Hillman Mary Nicholas Hill	Home:	Onondaga Castle, NY
		Clan:	Wolf
Early Schooling:	Thomas Indian School		
Later Schooling:			

experience with before coming to Carlisle. He didn't have any more outings during this enrollment after shifting to masonry.

Levi's first mention in a school publication was in October of 1907 when he played right halfback on the Painters football team. Listing the line-up for a shop team was highly unusual. As a result, we know little about the shop teams, including all of their names.

At the 1908 commencement ceremony, he received a Certificate in Plastering, Stone Cutting, and Cement Working. In February 1909, Levi spent three weeks in bed with pneumonia but recovered well. In June, he completed his enrollment and received an Industrial Certificate at commencement.

Levi returned as a member of the Senior Class on October 1, 1909 for a three-year enrollment after spending the summer at home. His father died while he was at Carlisle before. As Levi Hillman, he was elected Class Secretary. He received praise for how he delivered a declamation titled "Humility" at the opening ceremonies.

From this point on, he was referred to as Levi Hillman in Carlisle publications but not on official documents. His signature on documents signed after he left Carlisle tend to be as Levi Hillman. The Levi Hill portion appears to be very similar in both signatures, indicating that the government had his name wrong. It should have been Hillman not Hill.

In November 19 edition of *The Carlisle Arrow* his article, "The Walking Purchase," was published on the front page, above the fold. He described in detail how the white men cheated the Lenni Lenape on what was supposed to be a legitimate land purchase. Even after its founder Richard Henry Pratt was gone, the school had no difficulty discussing how Indians had been mistreated. One of its purposes was to educate them so they could fare better in future dealings.

During a December class meeting, he argued for the negative of "Resolved, That education has a greater influence than nature in the formation of character." His side won the debate as he "...proved himself to be an expert debater." He gave a talk "First" at the joint YMCA-YWCA meeting. The May 27, 1910 issue of *The Carlisle Arrow* included a piece he wrote about the Seneca creation story. After working the summer in Wilkes-Barre for George T. Dickover & Son

Levi is number 10, second row, second from the right.

brick manufacturers and contractors, Levi returned to Carlisle in late October to enroll in the Commercial course.

He never got into a varsity game but class members remembered his play:

> "To be sure the varsity eleven does not include any members of this athletic class, but nature alone must bear the responsibility for that; for in foot-ball; Lewis George and Levi Hillman both played successfully on the second eleven of the famous Carlisle foot-ball teams, and both were excellent players; but being very light, they were barred from the first eleven—a loss to

the varsity team that can hardly be estimated, in the opinion of 1910."

In February 1911, Levi served as a judge for a debate held at a special meeting of the Susan Longstreth Society. In March, he was elected treasurer of the Junior Commercial students. He spent the summer working for the same company as he had the previous summer. This year he returned three weeks earlier. The Standard Debating Society elected him treasurer and he participated in debates. In January 1912 he was elected vice-president. In May, he returned home, finished with his Carlisle education. He may have had a reason for leaving before the enrollment period was fulfilled.

On December 24, 1912 Levi Hillman, age 25, married Lovina George, age 18, by a local Justice of the Peace. This was the last document discovered on which the Hillman name was used. All future documents used Hill.

The 1915 New York State Census was the first document found to have July 7th as Levi's birthday. It also listed him as a mason and put daughter Evelyn's DOB at 1913. Levi Jr. came along three years later.

Something happened to Levi in 1919 that may have changed the course of his life. It all began when Robert Everingham picked up laundry Mrs. Hill had done for Everingham's mother. Lovina took offense with one of his comments then things escalated until she feared for her safety. She then told her husband what had happened. Apparently the boy departed without blows being thrown. A fracas involving Everingham and some Indians at a store in Rockwell Springs broke out on Saturday night marking the beginning of a race war. On Monday, Levi was ambushed by a group of marauding whites. "He was badly beaten...his face and body severely bruised and several deep gashes cut in his head. Stitches were needed to close one of the wounds."

When Dennison George was walking to the store to buy phonograph records, he was chased by a gang in an automobile. One of them knocked him to the ground by throwing a short length of water pipe at his legs. When he sought refuge with his sister Lovina, they took shots at the house. One of the shots just missed a visitor and three a young daughter's bedroom window.

Daughters Marion and Muriel arrived in 1920 and 1925, respectively. The family then lived in Nedrow, New York, formerly known as Onondaga Castle. Levi disappeared from the censuses for two decades. He did sign up for the World War II draft, listing his sister as the person who would always know his address. What happened to his wife is unknown.

He reappeared in 1948 as the victim of a severe beating. A passerby found him lying unconscious and called for help. He was taken to a hospital, where the laceration in his head required ten stitches. In 1955, Levi was convicted of public intoxication and sentenced to 60 days in jail. The next year he was sentenced to six months in the county penitentiary for striking a woman over the head with a kerosene lamp.

In 1958, Levi and a friend were attacked at 5 a.m. when two younger men broke into the friend's house and beat Levi and his friend severely with beer bottles over a supposed missing gallon of wine. He suffered a cut over the right eye and a broken nose. His friend got it worse.

The next year, Levi was found in a pool of his own blood badly beaten behind the Nedrow firehouse. He was admitted to intensive care with a fractured skull and serious bruising around his face and head. He recovered after a long stay in the hospital.

Levi died after a long illness in 1966. Son Levi Jr. and daughter Marion were his closest surviving relatives.

Louis Island

Louis Abraham Island was first enrolled at Carlisle some time in 1898. However, the records of that enrollment have been lost as has documentation of his birth, if such paperwork ever existed. Some family members believed he was born in Canada. He supplied Carlisle administrators 1890 as his birthyear but his widow had authorities put 1893 on his death certificate. Island was somewhere between five and eight years old when he first came to Carlisle. His older sister, Carrie, also attended Carlisle and was listed on the 1900 Federal census as being full-blood Oneida. Their father, also named Louis, was alive in 1905 to re-enroll his son for a second term, but their mother was deceased by that time. Like most small boys at Carlisle, he received little mention in the school newspaper during his early years at the school. His first mention in *The*

Name:	Louis A. Island	Nickname:	
DOB:	7/12/1890 or 7/12/1893	Height:	5'5"
Weight:	137 lbs.	Age:	21
Parents:	Louis Island Mary Cicle Island	Home:	Green Bay, WI
Early Schooling:	Oneida Boarding School likely		
Later Schooling:	Haskell Institute Chiropractic school		

Red Man and Helper listed him as one of the students returning from summer outing to start the new school term in September 1900. His next mention, over two years later, was when he scored a touchdown for the Blacksmiths in the shop championship game against the Printers.

Island became a Freshman in the fall of 1903, at which time he was elected president of the Class of 1907. Louis was very active in school affairs. He joined the Invincible Debating Society where he frequently spoke, participated in debates, and became an officer. After the 1905 football season was over, he was named to the school's "All-American Foot Ball team" at quarterback. Later in December, Louis participated in a gymnastics demonstration as part of the entertainment for a sociable. In December 1906, the Invincibles elected him president. Some time in his Carlisle career, Island shifted from blacksmithing to printing.

Though only 5'5¼" tall and weighing 148 pounds then, Louis made the varsity in 1906, playing quarterback behind Archie Libby. He got into the early games and onto the scoreboard by kicking a 30-yard field goal against Albright College. After that, his major playing time came with the Second Team. He drop-kicked a field goal against Dickinson Seminary in Williamsport, Pennsylvania but missed the kick after Theodore Owl's touchdown.

In the winter, Louis Island played left forward on the basketball team that represented Carlisle well against Franklin and Marshall College. In the spring, he played baseball on the school team. Somehow, he also found time to run track. He showed another side of his athletic prowess and chivalry at the Senior outing when he quickly donned a bathing suit to retrieve a purse a damsel dropped into the lake. A week later, he spoke at the local Methodist church he regularly attended. Staying at Carlisle over the summer, he pitched for the Printer's Devils against the Velvet Treaders, a team made of faculty and staff members, trouncing the elders 21–7.

Frank Mt. Pleasant was shifted back to quarterback in 1907, keeping Mike Balenti and Louis Island from moving up on the depth charts. Island and Balenti got into the early-season games and received good reviews. After the Villanova game, *The Arrow* reported, "His [Mt. Pleasant's] successor, Island, worked very creditably." *The Sentinel* echoed those sentiments: "Mt. Pleasant is better than ever in running with the ball and he handles the team well, although Island does as well in the latter respect as he." A couple of weeks later against Bucknell, the reports weren't as positive: "Mt. Pleasant was not in the game and Island filled his position most of the time, until replaced by Balenti. The former ran the team fairly well, but was poor on running back punts and was responsible for some heavy losses. Balenti was also weak in handling the ball. Both seemed to be anxious to get in the limelight by kicking drop-kicks, and Island did succeed in scoring in this manner." He also kicked a goal after touchdown. Filling in for a player who many thought should have received first team All-America honors is never easy, especially for players who would have been starters for most other teams. Because Mt. Pleasant was injured so badly in the Minnesota game, he had to sit out the big game with Chicago. Student reporter William Yankee Joe observed, "Every student thought that it was up to Island who has been backing up Mt. Pleasant during the season. But when we heard the line-up and with Balenti at quarter back some of the students were a little shaky." *The Arrow* thought those fears were unfounded: "Balenti and Island ran the play without a hitch, and the accurate kicking of Hauser, coupled with his slashing runs and line plunging, made up for the ground-gaining and scoring abilities of the regular quarter-back."

After football season, Louis focused his attention on his numerous other activities until graduation in April 1908. In addition to his diploma, he received an industrial certificate in Printing, Two-Thirds. Apparently, there was another third to the printing program. However, graduation from Carlisle didn't end his education.

In the fall of 1908, he enrolled at Haskell Institute. He also joined the football team. The purple and gold Fightin' Indians played such teams as Missouri, Texas, Nebraska, Texas A&M, LSU and Alabama. After two years in Kansas, 18-year-old Island returned to Wisconsin but thought of the Cumberland Valley.

From West DePere, Andrew Doxtator wrote Carlisle, "Louis Island is returned student and he wishes to go back to Carlisle again. This is all puples [sic] I could get." Island re-enrolled at Carlisle, this time in the commercial course, on September 10, 1910, and played football again. Again a solid player but not a star, Louis completed his career at the Indian school but remained nearby.

Island took a job at the Hershey Chocolate Company, which made visits to campus practical. On March 17, 1911, *The Arrow* reported that Louis and William Newashe, also employed at Hershey, played on the Hershey YMCA basketball team against their old school.

Their old classmates loudly applauded their pluck. In May the *Harrisburg Telegraph* announced Louis's registration as a student at Lebanon Valley College in Annville, Pennsylvania.

In the fall of 1913, he started his professional football career playing end for the Jackson, Michigan All-Stars or Independents, as they were sometimes called. Made up largely of University of Michigan players no longer eligible because of grades or other infractions, the Independents were a competitive team. In fact, they claimed the southern Michigan championship until defeated by the Fort Wayne Friars in a game played in a snowstorm on the Friars' home field, League Park, in Fort Wayne, Indiana. The Friars were so impressed by Island they hired him for the 1914 season. He played well enough to be brought back in 1915. The Friars went 7-1-1 with him playing right end and quarterback. He would have likely been back for another season, but an off-field accident ended his playing career.

At some point, Louis located in Fort Wayne and took a job as a punch-press operator at the local General Electric plant. In his spare time, he officiated whatever game was in season for area teams. In early May 1916, his left thumb was crushed in a punch-press accident. Island lost the best part of a month's work due to the injury but returned to the same job in late May.

That fall, Louis began his coaching career by taking charge of the West End junior team. Because the West End of Fort Wayne, now a historic district, was populated by many of the movers and shakers of the town, Island very likely coached the scions of important families and made contacts that would serve him well in the future. At the beginning of the season, pundits considered it the strongest team West End ever fielded. Louis's team played well most of the season but lost their last regular-season game to the rival Badgers, throwing the city junior championship into turmoil with three teams making claims to it. Once the season ended, he began officiating basketball games and continued doing that through the winter. He had arranged a nice life for a bachelor: he had a job that covered his living expenses and in his free time he participated in his first love—sports. This idyllic life was rudely interrupted by events thousands of miles away across the Atlantic.

The June 27, 1917 edition of *The Fort Wayne Sentinel* crowed, "When Battery D [sic] leaves here the latter part of this week or the first of next week its roll will include the name of one of the best athletes of the city, Louis Island. Louis went to headquarters last night and signed

up, ready to do his bit as a true American wherever the unit may be ordered...When he leaves the city it will be with the best wishes of a host of friends and admirers." That day's *Fort Wayne Journal-Gazette* gave him a send off: "Believing that he, a true American, should 'do his bit,' Louis Island, the well-known football player, appeared at Battery B recruiting headquarters last night and signed up for service with the artillery...Island should make good with the battery as he had four years' infantry training at Carlisle. It is a sure thing that if he plays the artillery game as hard as he did the gridiron game there are bound to be some German lines smashed and a few plays broken up. Here's to you, Louis, and success."

Three days later, *The Fort Wayne Daily News* reported that Pvt. Island was given the honor of carrying the unit's flag. The flag was purchased with funds raised by contributions collected by Mrs. F. H. Banks. "Lieutenant L. F. Woods received the flag and then handed it to Private Louis Island, saying that he knew of no one in the battery more worthy to carry the colors." About six weeks later, *The Journal-Gazette* covered a parade: "When Battery B paraded yesterday as United States regulars, Fred Fosmire, of German and Irish parentage, and Louis Island, a full-blooded Indian, carried the Stars and Stripes and artillery guidon. Thus does Americanism unite all under the flag in common service to the nation." On August 16, Louis A. Island was promoted to the rank of sergeant. It isn't known if the fact that 18 men failing the physical examination affected his promotion.

Battery B shipped over to France, arriving in November 1917, as a component of the 150th United States Field Artillery of the Rainbow Division. He was engaged in fighting at Chateau Thierry, Verdun, second battle of the Marne, St. Mihiel, and the Argonne, where he was on the firing line when the armistice was signed. He accompanied the army of occupation into Germany and was stationed at Coblenz until sent home. In April 1919, Sgt. Island and seven others, one of whom was dead, were cited for "especial bravery" for serving the guns while under fire during the American drive at Chateau Thierry. The May 11 *Journal-Gazette* praised him with the headline, "Friar Grid Star Is Welcomed Home With Batteries B and D." A photo of him accompanied the article. "Loie, we greet you. May you live long and prosper."

And that was exactly what he intended to do. Soon Louis Island's name was showing up again on the sports page for coaching football. He continued his life of working at mundane jobs while coaching and officiating on the side until the late 1920s. His employment history during this time included working as a gardener and as a meter man.

But in 1928, he had no occupation. This likely meant he was attending a professional school to better his position in life because the next year he was listed on the Fort Wayne city directory as being a chiropractor. The 1930 census listed his occupation as drugless physician, which was likely another term for chiropractor at the time. Indiana didn't license chiropractors until 1955, so he may have been practicing under

Louis Island's graduation from chiropractic school

some other title. In some states, chiropractors practiced as drugless physicians to avoid going to jail for practicing medicine without a license, which happened to some of those who called themselves chiropractors.

Louis & Phoebe Island

Dr. Island, as he was now called, had made a major life change in the early 1920s. He married a white woman named Phoebe Harsh from Mentone, Indiana. Phoebe was a farm girl who had four sisters but no brothers. So, Louis was the only young male at family gatherings for a time. Niece Iris Davis and nephew Dick Boganwright knew him only as small children but recall that he was "a nice, friendly guy" who liked children. Outgoing without being loud Louis was soon Outgoing without being loud, Louis was soon well thought of by Phoebes family. He and Phoebe had a son, Harsh Louis Island. Just as Louis had settled into a career and family life, the unexpected struck. In September 1933, Dr. Island died of tuberculosis. Phoebe lived 22 years more. Their son, who was also known as Louis, died young as had his father. His death was thought to be caused by an infection of a wound acquired in the Korean War.

Emerson Metoxen

Numerous members of the Metoxen (believed to have been Met-the-oxen originally) family attended Carlisle Indian School. Emerson at Carlisle on September 26, 1914, age 15, to begin a three-year enrollment at the school. Too young to try out for the varsity, he probably played on one of the several intramural football teams. He joined the Boy Scout troop on campus and soon completed the requirements for Second Class. He was also initiated into the Standard Debating Society. In the spring the Boy Scouts promoted him to First Class.

In August 1915, Emerson suffered an appendix attack which required surgery. That diagnosis triggered a series of letters from the

Name:	Emerson Metoxen	Nickname:	Chief
DOB:	4/23/1899	Height:	5'9"
Weight:	158 lbs.	Age:	15
Parents:	Nelson Metoxen	Home:	Oneida, WI
	Louisa Metoxen (deceased)	Clan:	Turtle
Early Schooling:	Oneida Indian School		
	Tomah Indian School		
Later Schooling:	Mercersburg Academy		
	Lebanon Valley College		
	Harvard University		

physician up the bureaucracy and out to the reservation and to Emerson's father to get permission to operate. Dr. Rendtorff operated on the morning of September 7. On September 14, the superintendent forwarded the physician's report to Emerson's father:

> "I am glad to report that the present writing finds Emerson Metoxen sitting up in bed. There is still considerable discharge of pus from the abdomen but the boy's general condition is excellent."

The surgery was successful, allowing Emerson to return to his school activities. Little was written about his activities that school year, possibly because his recuperation kept him on the sidelines for sports. He spent the summer of 1916 waiting tables for Joseph Oliver at Camp Pokanoket on Lake Carey, a resort in Wyoming County, Pennsylvania along with two other Carlisle students.

In October, he gave an impromptu speech at a Standards meeting. That winter Emerson starred at basketball, scoring 23 of the team's points in a 47-39 loss in Carlisle's season opener with Lebanon Valley College. Later in December, he successfully argued the negative against the proposition "That the President of the United States should be elected by a direct vote of the people." He continued making hoops as a forward on the basketball team until spring, when he made the varsity lacrosse team. Beating perennial lacrosse power Johns Hopkins 6-2 started Carlisle's season with a bang, portending the good season they had.

Emerson spent the summer working at Camp Greylock, a boys camp "In the heart of the Berkshires" near Becket, Massachusetts. He earned a $50 salary plus $38 gratuities. The fall of 1917 found Emerson on the varsity football team, playing tailback (left halfback) on the second string. He made several long gains playing much of the second half in the season opener, a 60-0 shellacking of Albright College. The youngest and lightest team ever field by Carlisle then took Franklin & Marshall College 63-0 for an auspicious start to the season. The tide abruptly shifted the next week with a 21-0 loss to West Virginia at Morgantown. A 61-0 keelhauling by Navy followed that. A 15-7 win over Johns Hopkins was their last victory of the season.

The 1917 Carlisle Indians football team

They didn't score a single point the rest of the year. The only high point was a tour of West Point when they played Army, about which Emerson gave a talk to Room 12 about the trip. A low point had to be his writing up an account of the season-ending 26-0 drubbing by rival Penn for the school paper.

As busy as ever that winter and spring, Emerson was elected Historian for the Standard Debating Society and he lettered in both basketball and lacrosse. At the end of the school year in June, his older sister Sadie graduated and he returned home to Wisconsin, his enrollment period fulfilled. On July 13, he wrote Nellie Denny at Carlisle, requesting admission forms for a brother and sister, Pearson and Cecilia, and a subscription to the school newspaper for himself. He also wrote about his work at the shipyard in Manitowoc.

Nellie responded on July 16, stating she was sending the requested forms and she promised to send him the yearbook as soon as it came off the press. The school newspaper was in summer hiatus at that time. She also promised to have train tickets arranged for his return to

Carlisle Indians' Crack Lacrosse Team Closes the Season With Only One Defeat and Promises Better Record For Next Year

Top Row—Left to right, Clyde M. Bair, manager; J. Holstein, first defense; F. Walker, cover point; C. Walker, third defence; Jake Herman, substitute; W. Washington, second defense; P. Norl, captain, out home; William O'Neill, coach. Middle Row—Ira Cloud, home; Emerson Metoxen, third attack; E. Wright, substitute; Guy Elm, substitute. Lower Row—G. Cushing, first attack; W. Large, substitute; L. Bruner, goal; N. Hayes, center; Clement Vigil, second attack.

Carlisle to reenroll. Emerson wasn't to return to his studies at Carlisle and his younger sister and brother couldn't enroll because Carlisle Indian School closed on August 31, 1918 The Army took over Carlisle Barracks the next day to set up a hospital to treat soldiers wounded in France. Emerson didn't return for many years. His younger brother Pearson was to have a fine athletic career just not at Carlisle.

Emerson's employment at the shipyard must have been a summer job because, when he registered for the draft in September, he listed "Nothing" in the space for his present job. He appeared to be living at home at the time.

A November 7 newspaper article listed him among the several men selected to entrain for Camp Logan at Houston, Texas on November 11. However, he had already qualified for induction into the Navy as a hospital corpsman. The fighting may have ended on November 11 but thousands of men, many of whom were wounded or sick, had to be transported back to the United States. One supposes he had to undergo training before he could be assigned to a ship. The government commandeered the German luxury liner *Imperator* for use as a transport ship and assigned Emerson to its crew. One may conclude from his induction rating that his job was to treat the sick and wounded on their trips home across the Atlantic. The *Imperator* was retired from its wartime duties in September 1919 after transporting 25,000 troops,

SS *Imperator*

nurses, and civilians back to the U. S. In November its ownership was transferred jointly to the Cunard and White Star Lines as war reparations for sinking the *Lusitania* and renamed *Berengia*.

After his discharge from the Navy, Emerson enrolled at Mercersburg Academy, a prep school located south of Carlisle down the Cumberland Valley near the Maryland border. He didn't get enough playing time in the 1920 football season to letter but was awarded the honor of wearing the "AMA," a step down from the Mercersburg "M."

The next fall, 1921, found Emerson enrolled at Lebanon Valley College in Annville, Pennsylvania. Although he was in the prep school, he was allowed to play on the varsity teams. He got into the 33-0 loss to Army as a substitute fullback. He didn't get into the 21-21 tie with Muhlenberg College the next Saturday but he did sign the letter to *The Patriot-News* vindicating the honor of referee Eberle who was knocked unconscious after the game by Muhlenberg supporters and held Muhlenberg responsible for the actions of their fans and rooters. He missed several games due to injury but was healthy enough for the season-ending Susquehanna University contest on Thanksgiving Day. He got in late in the game at fullback in the 2-0 loss, with the only score being a first-quarter safety on a misplayed punt. He got enough playing time in football and basketball games to letter in both sports.

In early April, Emerson fell out for baseball practice every day as a catcher in spite of the rainy weather and soggy diamond. He caught a one-hitter and batted ninth in the 1922 season opener, a 1-0 shutout at home against Franklin & Marshall College. He was hitless again in a 14-5 loss to Juniata College. He committed three errors in a 5-1 pasting by Susquehanna. Emerson's hitless streak continued in a 5-2 loss to

Bucknell. Emerson scored two runs in a 15-6 win at Dickinson College. In a 6-3 rematch victory over against Susquehanna, he got a hit. His two passed balls helped Gettysburg College beat the Dutchmen 10-6, putting them back below .500. He sat out the 1-0 shutout of Blue Ridge College, possibly because of his performance against Gettysburg. His backup, Wolfe, caught for the second game in a row, a 1-0 win over Dickinson College. Emerson returned to the line-up against Ursinus with a bang, slapping out two singles and a double and scoring a run while making no errors in the 5-4 win. Wolfe caught in the 6-2 loss to Villanova. Metoxen caught the rematch against Villanova but was lifted for a pinch hitter in the 7th inning of the 4-2 loss. He got no hits but made no errors in the 2-0 shutout at Juniata College to close LVC's erratic season and end the school year.

Emerson and Wilfred Perry signed with the Hartford Senators of the Eastern League to play summer ball. Their names weren't listed on the team's roster, but they may have played under assumed names as many college boys did.

That fall Emerson developed the skill of drop kicking, something his coach appreciated. He made good yardage against Penn in a preseason scrimmage. An overly optimistic schedule led to successive losses to Army, Georgetown, and Penn State, setting LVC up for a losing 1922 season. Four successive wins over St. Josephs, Washington, Juniata, and Susquehanna put them over .500—briefly. Losses to Lehigh and Gettysburg sealed LVC's fate. Players were listed in the yearbook only as first year, second year, etc., not as freshman, etc. Emerson's name wasn't in class listings but some digging found it buried in a small section titled "Sub-Freshmen and Specials" below the listings of those in the Conservatory of Music.

Emerson was again the basketball team's best shooter but practicing on an undersized home court put LVC's cagers at a disadvantage when playing on regulation courts. A disappointing season resulted.

Baseball found Emerson behind the plate as usual. "His alertness and batting turned not a few defeats into victories." They won one more game than they lost in Coach "Pop" Kelchner's last season.

In the fall of 1923, Emerson was listed as a sophomore playing end on a football team that had a new coach. Scheduling powers such as

Army, Penn State, and Holy Cross put a winning season out of reach. They finished a little better than the previous year at 4-4-1.

Emerson shined again at basketball with improved dribbling skills added to his dead-eye shooting. Unfortunately, he wasn't enough to carry the team to a winning season.

He anchored the baseball team behind the plate. "Because of his alertness and his powerful right arm he always had the base runner at his mercy." The 1924 baseball team finished with a 9-5 record.

Metoxen didn't play football in 1924. Perhaps he was injured as the yearbook entry for his basketball play suggested. Or, he was having academic issues as the yearbook listed him in the Special Students section under Conservatory Students.

Emerson captained the 1924-25 basketball team. With only three returning lettermen, the team struggled to a losing record. "Although 'Chief' was not up to his usual standard he acted like a real leader and under his guidance the team fought many hard battles, and through his inspiration succeeded in trimming out old rivals, Albright."

The 1925 baseball season found him at his usual position yet again. The team played a longer scheduled than usual and came out on the long end of 12-6 for Emerson's last year.

He played end again on the 1925 LVC football team. They had a disappointing 2-3-3 season losing more games than they won as well as tying more. The 1927 yearbook listed him as a Senior but didn't include his photograph.

In October 1925, the Oneidas installed Emerson as a Principal Chief of the Turtle Clan. He was now officially a chief, an honorarium which he had been unofficially bestowed by sportswriters for years.

He captained the 1926 basketball team to an 8-9 season. It was less disappointing than it might have been because they only played three home games.

During baseball practice in April, Emerson took ill. When his fever reached 103, he was admitted to the Lebanon Sanatorium. The reason for his high temperature turned out to be the measles. He lost the entire month of April to this disease. When he returned, Metoxen played right field and the team went 7-7 for a .500 season.

In May, Emerson was elected to represent his class in the Men's Senate.

He played end again on the 1926 football team that went 4-4 for the season. Having used up his basketball eligibility, he had to sit out that season. He used some of his free time to officiate high school games. He also put together a team of former players, called Metoxen's Indians, to play against local independent teams.

The 1927 baseball season was progressing well for Emerson until he broke the thumb on his right hand tagging a runner at home plate. His thumb had recovered enough to pinch hit for Piela in the ninth in a losing contest against Albright College on Memorial Day. He was able to catch the entire game for the loss to Penn State on June 3 to complete the season with an 8-5 record.

After graduating with a B. S. in Education, Emerson took a summer job as athletic instructor at Camp Namaschaug on Lake Spofford in New Hampshire. In mid-July, he had to interrupt his work there to travel 200 miles to New York City for an interview for a position at York Collegiate Institute (YCI) in York, Pennsylvania. He was offered the job and he accepted. His duties included teaching biology and serving as the school's physical director. As physical director he also coached sports.

With no football team at YCI at the time, his coaching duties started with the basketball team. He inherited four starters from the previous year's team and built his team around them. Their season started with a bang, holding Columbia High School scoreless for the first 37 minutes, winning 74-4! Next up would be a real test:

York Collegiate Institute 1874

Dickinson College freshmen. The loss of six-foot center Joe Baker to injury made competing all-the-more difficult for Metoxen's men. However, the college boys proved to be little stronger than YCI's first opponent, giving the Orange and White another overwhelming victory: 59-14.

Emerson also coached the J. V. team, which played a schedule separate from that of the varsity. They won their first game 39-9 over Stewartstown High School. The third game for the varsity was against the alumni. The "point-a-Minute" boys beat their elders 56-21 ending their contests for the calendar year.

1928 started with a more intensive schedule, with one or two games to be played each week. Joe Baker had healed and was ready to play the first game of the new year. Metoxen's charges humbled powerhouse Central High School of Washington, DC 61-20 to christen York's White Rose Arena before a large crowd. The arena manager had workers toiling until 11:00 p.m. readying the new facility for its first use.

Next up was Perkiomen School of Pennsburg, their first conference foe for the season. YCI emerged victorious after a hard-fought game: 44-32. Joe Baker score 27 points in the 61-39 win over Gettysburg College freshmen. For the first time this year an opposing team outscored YCI in a half by the Bullets scoring 28 to YCI's 24 in the second stanza.

Mining and Mechanical Institute (MMI) of Freeland, Pennsylvania fought hard but got walloped 49-26. Wyoming Seminary two nights later proved to be YCI's toughest foes so far with YCI emerging a 27-23 winner. With an 11-point lead late in the game YCI tried to run out the clock but Wyoming took advantage and closed the gap to just four points. YCI was now at 3-0, atop Eastern Prep School League standings.

The next week, YCI humbled previously undefeated Allentown Prep 36-10. Missed free throws kept the score closer than it should have been. YCI trailed at half time for the first time in their game at Gettysburg College. They rebounded in the second half to overcome the freshmen 36-29. Then they defeated the University of Pennsylvania freshmen 42-30 for YCI's seventh straight win over the Quakers.

Having their cars slide into the ditch on the way to Pennsburg didn't dampen YCI's iron nerve, which aided them in eking out a 44-41 win over Perkiomen. Their next opponent, Franklin & Marshall College Academy (F&M), presented little trouble. Metoxen's subs played throughout the 70-27 wipeout for YCI's 16th straight win. Speedy guard Harry Baxter wasn't needed while he was confined with tonsilitis.

Coach Metoxen used a flurry of players, most of whom were kept on the floor for short bursts Friday night against MMI, in what must have been an attempt to keep his players fresh for the big tournament the next day. YCI still won easily, 53-30.

YCI hoped to repeat winning the annual University of Pennsylvania Interscholastic Basketball Tournament held at The Palestra in Philadelphia. Originally, they were scheduled to play Pennsylvania Institution for the Deaf (PID) at 2:00 p.m. on Saturday. Not wanting to get his players out of bed at 5:00 a.m. to catch a train after having played a game the night before, Emerson implored tournament officials for a later start time. He thought it unfair considering Philadelphia teams weren't scheduled to play until Monday. PID withdrew from the tournament, causing some to assume YCI would then get a first-round bye. That didn't happen. They just substituted a different opponent for PID in the same time slot. Emerson caved and the team played without bedridden Baxter. They took care of their first opponent, Rutgers Preparatory School (RPS), with ease, winning 36-12.

Their second-round game was played on Tuesday against Cook Academy of New Jersey. Cook presented YCI its toughest opposition to date, keeping Baker scoreless from the floor, and forcing overtime for YCI to prevail 22-21. In the semifinals, YCI faced the same team they faced the previous year before Metoxen came to YCI. Hun School of Princeton gave them few problems. Winning 32-23, YCI proceeded to the finals against St. Johns of Manlius, New York. Three years earlier, the Manlius School (as they were called) put them out of the tournament. Not so under Metoxen. His boys won 32-14 to bring the trophy back to York again, extending their string of victories to 45 straight wins.

YCI completed its regular season with a tight game with Wyoming Seminary. The score was 21-20 at the end of the third quarter but YCI pulled away for a 32-26 victory, remaining unbeaten for both the conference and the season with just two regularly scheduled games remaining.

Against F&M Academy at Lancaster, Emerson rotated his players throughout the game to keep them fresh. Captain Ullrich was held out until late in the first half due to an abscessed tooth that fortunately didn't hurt his shooting. Lowell and Miller's sharpshooting wasn't enough to keep the score close. Not close at all at 51-29.

YCI had a history of sending the scrubs to play Columbia High School but this year's contract required them to guarantee the regular line-up or lose the expense money. Even though Emerson alternated the regulars with JV players, the closest Columbia got was 36-13 at the end of the 3rd quarter. The final score was 51-16.

Not satisfied going unbeaten and winning the Penn tournament, Metoxen signed the team up for the Eastern United States Invitational Tournament at Glenn Falls, New York. Before accepting the invitation, he had toyed with the idea of playing a couple more games before closing down for the year. After accepting, he decided against it. "The boys need a rest and have been forbidden to go to a basketball court this week. Too much basketball is just as harmful as not enough sometimes." They returned to work the early part of the week of the tournament.

Peekskill Military Academy of New York succumbed 37-32 for a first-round victory foy YCI. Next up was Wilby High School of Waterbury, Connecticut. Wilby proved to be no match for YCI, losing 37-22. For the championship[p, YCI doubled up Rogers High School of Newport, Rhode Island 28-14. Emerson continued the winning streak his predecessor started, maintaining the prestige of the program. The local press called this "Greatest Season In History of School Ends Triumphantly" and the players "Wonder Team." Metoxen was called "A Real Leader."

After seeing the tournament game, Coach Killeher of Fordham wrote Emerson, congratulating him on his team's play and offered Ullrich, McKinstry, MacNiff, and Kane the opportunity to enroll at Fordham after the end of the school year.

Emerson returned after Easter break to start get the track team ready to compete in the Penn Relays on April 28. YCI canceled at the last minute for unstated reasons and stayed home.

On May 5 in conjunction with Boys Week, Emerson was in complete charge of the archery event. He also gave a talk on health at William Penn Senior High as part of Boys Week. He left York in mid-July to again serve as an athletic instructor at Camp Namaschaug until the beginning of September.

CYI opened the 1928-29 school year with the record enrollment of 195 pupils, with 59 in the primary department, 39 in the intermediate department, and the rest in the first through sixth forms. Emerson was put in charge of the new school store which would be operated on a nonprofit basis.

CYI had disbanded its football team after the 1909 season but Emerson wanted to revive the sport. He was allocated the funds for the necessary equipment but didn't have a field on which to play home games. Putting together a schedule in late-September wasn't an easy task. All he could do was to arrange games for dates other schools had left open.

Emerson's younger brother Pierson, who didn't have the opportunity to attend Carlisle Indian School, lined up at center for their first game, which was played at Harrisburg Academy. It ended with a disputed score. An official denied a safety when the Academy's punt returned was tackled in the end zone, calling it a touchback instead. No other points were scored. York papers claimed it was a 2-0 YCI win.

A 26-point second quarter propelled YCI over Elizabethtown High School, 32-6. Emerson moved his brother from center to left halfback. Long runs by him and Meister were keys to the victory. YCI's next win was a 27-0 romp over Nottingham Academy of Colora, Maryland. No other games could be arranged after this, so Coach Metoxen put football in his rearview, until the next year anyway, and shifted his focus on basketball.

He arranged a schedule similar to the previous year, except for adding three tough opponents. Due to graduations, Emerson installed a practically new starting five. He assigned Pierson to the JV. The varsity began the season by smothering York Catholic 67-15. The next week they played the alumni, this time essentially last year's undefeated team. The alumni kept it close for three quarters but the youngsters outscored them 10-2 in the final stanza. YCI built a 13-point lead over the first three quarters against the Lebanon Valley College freshmen before fading in the fourth. Their lead was too much to overcome so they hung on for the 34-29 win before Christmas break.

1929 started on a low note with Calvert Hall of Baltimore breaking YCI's 55-game winning streak 37-36. Kane's last-second basket wasn't counted because he didn't get the shot off in time. YCI's lightning shuttle passing overcame the Villanova freshmen putting YCI back on track 34-21. Former YCI stars Freddie Ullrich and Mickie MacNiff led the University of Pennsylvania freshmen in a 37-25 defeat of their old school, outscoring them in every quarter. Calvert Hall refused to give YCI a rematch "...owing to a hard schedule..."

YCI bounced back against Wyoming Academy 34-27 by opening up a lead after being tied at halftime. They demolished Freeland MMI 69-22, showing great teamwork. The Orange and White barely got by Wyoming Seminary by a last second shot from the corner by Tony Wilkins, winning 31-29. They were now 7-0 in conference. Freeland MMI played considerably better at home than in York, tying YCI at the end of the third quarter. The visitors won by holding the home team to two points in the fourth quarter, ending the game 37-33. Perkiomen wasn't easy either. YCI had to overcome a double-digit deficit before winning going away, 35-21. They broke Georgetown freshmen's 14-game winning streak by defeating them convincingly 33-17.

YCI began their defense of the Penn Tournament title with a 32-23 defeat of Berkshire School of Pittsfield, Massachusetts. Next up was Cook, a team they had played the year before. This year they seemed helpless at times against the Cook cagers, losing 30-17. Their last game and loss was to Hun School 26-25 in the first round of the Glen Falls tournament. They won their conference championship again but failed to defend either of the tournament titles they had won the year before. For the second year in a row, YCI did not send a team to the Penn Relays.

For most, this would have been a successful season but Emerson had loftier goals. In May, he had his new 1929 Chevrolet stolen at gunpoint. He got it back quickly but the thief had damaged it in a collision with the local prosecutor. Later that month, the 17-year-old perpetrator was sent to the Huntingdon reformatory for the robbery charges, sentenced to 90 days in the York County jail, and fined $200 plus cost for operating an automobile under the in fluence of alcohol. No mention was made of restitution for the damages done to the cars he damaged.

York County Academy was merged into York Collegiate Institute that fall. Classes began on September 11 with an estimated enrollment of 200 students. Emerson was able to arrange five games for the football team's 1929 season, all of which were to be played on the opponents' fields.

In the disastrous first game, Jacob Tome Institute at Port Deposit, Maryland demolished CYI's inexperienced team 58-0. The second game was worse, a 90-0 thrashing by Harrisburg Academy. Franklin & Marshall Academy rung up its first win by defeating the much lighter YCI team 33-0. Metoxen's charges finally scored and won on their fourth try. They beat Nottingham Academy 32-0. The one-game winning streak fizzled the following Saturday when Shippensburg State Teachers College Reserves beat them 27-0 for their closest loss, ending the dismal season.

Emerson shifted gears and laid out a 16-game basketball schedule for the 1929-30 season, including eleven home games. YCI dropped out of the Easter Pennsylvania Preparatory School League because it was a losing financial proposition and lacked competitive rivals. All games on the schedule would be against prep schools and college freshmen squads.

In what must have been a warm-up game for the season, YCI destroyed Gulf Refining Company 70-19. They started 1930 off beating Harrisburg Academy 42-19. Pennsylvania Business College didn't put up much of a fight, losing to YCI 60–10. Dickinson College freshmen went down 40-24 at Carlisle, for YCI's seventh straight win and first road of the season. They next ground out a gritty 27-23 win over Perkiomen. Harrisburg Academy couldn't defend against YCI's fast passing and went down 37-21. Metoxen's boys came from behind late to beat Gettysburg Academy on the Eddie Plank gym floor 37-33.

Emerson tendered his resignation two days later, effective the end of the school term when his three-year contract would be completed. He did not have a new position arranged at the time. YCI then defeated Franklin & Marshall Academy at Lancaster, 35-27. They defeated Dickinson College freshmen 26-12 in spite of poor foul shooting. YCI extended its winning streak to 14 games by defeating the Gettysburg College freshmen again 26-17. The played Gettysburg Academy, their most feared local opponent next. After playing a close first half, they pulled away for a 45-28 win that was tougher than the score indicated. They closed their regular season with a second win over Franklin & Marshall Academy, jolting them 36-20.

At the Palestra in Philadelphia as a preliminary before Penn's big game against Columbia, YCI defeated the Penn freshmen 29-27 in overtime. It was a dark night for the Quakers, losing both contests. As a preparation for the Glen Falls tournament, YCI took on Valley Forge Military Academy, winning a close one 28-25 at York Senior High.

At the Glen Falls Tournament, they lost their first-round game to the defending national champions, Cook Academy of Montour Falls, New York 27-24.

Two undefeated regular seasons out of three for Emerson wasn't bad. Why the school awarded him a gold watch is unclear. He was far from retirement age and had only worked at YCI for three years.

That summer, 1930, he attended a course at Harvard in advanced coaching. In September, he accepted a position at Swarthmore Preparatory School as head baseball coach and assistant coach for football and basketball. Pierson enrolled and played fullback on the varsity football team. Emerson led the undefeated JV team to eight victories. At the end of the season, he was made director of athletics in charge of all sports.

At the end of basketball season in March 1931, Emerson married Kathryn Jacobs of York, Pennsylvania in Bel Air, Maryland. Why would they have gotten married in Maryland instead of Pennsylvania? At that time Maryland was the Las Vegas of the East because it had no waiting period. Bel Air was not far south of the state line, making it a convenient spot for Pennsylvania runaways. Why would they have run away? Her family may have objected to her marrying an Indian, even though he had proven himself to be an upstanding citizen. Prejudices against inter-racial marriages were common at that time. It was likely Kathryn's Pennsylvania divorce from Arthur Adair did not allow her to remarry. She had returned to using her maiden name but retained custody of her son Arthur Jr.

That summer, Emerson attended another coaching course at Harvard. In the fall, he took a teaching position at Glen-Nor High School, which served neighboring towns Glenolden and Norwood. Now having a family to support, he probably needed more income than he got from prep schools. Blocked kicks proved to be Glen-Nor's downfall in their 12-0 season-opening loss to Berwyn High. Their next game, played against Haverford High, went even worse. Having no answer for Haverford's aerial attack, Glen-Nor went down 34-0. Glen-Nor's contest against Downingtown High ended as a scoreless tie. The next Friday they played another scoreless tie, this time with Nether Providence High School. They finally scored against Prospect Park High School but lost 26-6. This was the first touchdown scored by the school in two years. Glen-Nor battled Swarthmore High to another scoreless tie although both teams had chances to score. Glen-Nor made its first extra point of the year in its 19-7 loss to Collingdale High School. The 7-0 loss to Media High School was the result of a fourth quarter interception deep in Glen-Nor's territory. The 14-0 loss to Eddystone High continued the winless season. Ridley Park High ran roughshod over hapless Glen-Nor in their 40-0 Thanksgiving Day thrashing, bringing the winless season to a merciful end. Emerson was pleased with the development of his players.

His basketball players' season didn't start any better. They lost their first game 29-6 to Collingdale. In January, Eddystone won on two late baskets, 28-24. Glen-Nor bounced back against Berwick, 29-27 after three overtimes. Things looked bright with the game against Marple-Newtown High tied at the end of the third quarter but the "Pikers" never scored again in their 26-20 loss. They then lost a battle to get out of last place in the league to Swarthmore High, 19-15. A mid-week 25-13 victory over Ridley Park improved their record. A 38-18 win over P:rospect Park was sparked by a 23-point second half. They then trimmed Berwyn High in a Tuesday game, 32-22. They lost to Eddystone after closing the score in the second half 22-20. A 21-19 win over Ridley Park had to cheer up Emerson. They then won a low-scoring game against Swarthmore High 14-10. They scored a lot more in a 35-20 win over Prospect Park. They lost to Haverford 24-19 in the Kiwanis Tournament after being blanked in the fourth quarter. Emerson had to be happy with the improvement the team made in the second half of the season.

Emerson had four experienced backs and four experience linemen around which to build his 1932 team. The season-opening game against Haverford was canceled because school openings were postponed due to the infantile paralysis (polio) scare. Two safeties and two touchdowns doomed Glen-Nor to defeat against Downingtown High, 16-0, starting the season on a low note. Glen-Nor finally got a win at Nether Providence via an aerial attack, taking down the home team 12-6. The next week, Prospect Park rained on their parade 13-0. Swarthmore High got by them 14-7. Collingdale High's inability to convert an extra point try late in the game allowed Glen-Nor to squeak by 14-13 for their second win of the year. Another missed extra point gave them the margin of victory over winless Media High, 7-6. Media had the ball first and goal at the Glen-Nor 3-yard-line when time expired. So, this was a second straight squeaker. Ridley Park won the annual Thanksgiving game 19-6. A 3-4-0 season my not sound great but it was a tremendous improvement over 1931 and the losses weren't total blow outs as several were in 1931.

Basketball season started with a 24-20 win over Swarthmore High. Emerson led the faculty with a basket and a brace of free throws in a 26-6 loss to the varsity.

Glen-Nor defeated Berwyn High 24-5, shutting out the visitors in the second half of an after-school game to kick off the 1933 portion of their season. Emerson's boys suffered their first loss of the season 27-16 to Collingdale. The varsity lost to Ridley Park 21-11 and the Second Team lost to Ridley Park's Second Team 19-12. The varsity lost again. This time to Eddystone, 23-13. They bounced back with a 16-7 defeat of Swarthmore High. The February 7 game with Prospect Park was postponed. In the next game, they knocked Collingdale out of the top of the league standings 23-21. Then they overwhelmed Berwyn 30-19.

Ridley Park pounded them 27-14 to stay at the top of league standings. Eddystone knocked Glen-Nor out of third place, 34-19. In post-season play, Glen-Nor knocked Prospect Park out of the Kiwanis Delaware County Tournament with good defensive work, 24-4. In the second round they lost a heartbreaker 19-18 to Chester High.

Now in the depths of the Great Depression in 1933, Glen-Nor teacher salaries were cut two and a half to ten percent, administrators ten percent. Being relatively new at Glen-Nor, Emerson's pay cut would likely have been closer to the low end of the range. The teaching staff went unpaid in June due to the lack of tax receipts. This would have surely pinched Emerson because he and his wife had had a baby girl in October. Tax revenue must have come in because the school was ready to reopen on schedule in September.

Prospects for the 1933 football team were rosy. A number of veterans turned out for the first practice and he had three experienced football men for assistants. Emerson boasted that his team would rule the Chester Pike.

Fumbles destroyed any chance Glen-Nor had of winning their opener, a 20-0 loss to Berwyn. A 7-6 win over Sharon Hill evened the ledger. A 98-yard punt return was all the scoring Glen-Nor needed to beat Downingtown 6-2. In a game a successful extra point would have won, Glen-Nor tied Nether Providence 12-12. Prospect Park laced them 30-8 in a rivalry game. Glen-Nor dropped below .500 with a 7-6 loss to Swarthmore High. Collingdale soured Emerson's hopes for a good season 25-0. Glen-Nor responded with a 47-0 shellacking of Marple-Newtown. A 25-0 Thanksgiving Day thumping brought an end to the disappointing season. Perhaps basketball would be better.

Second-half shooting enabled Glen-Nor to overwhelm Collingdale 33-20 to start 1934 off on the right foot. Then Marple-Newtown went down 34-10. Eddystone fell next 24-14. Metoxen's boys blew a 2-point halftime lead to lose 33-19 to Haverford High School at South Ardmore. Then Swarthmore High rained on their parade 17-15. Collingdale extended their losing streak by defeating them 25-19, and knocking them out of first place in their division. A 20-18 loss to Eddystone dropped them to fourth place. Glen-Nor upset Prospect Park 36-23 at Prospect Park to right the ship. A 40-25 whipping of

Sharon Hill surely put a smile back on Edison's face. A 20-19 nailbiter against Upper Darby moved Glen-Nor into a second-place tie with Prospect Park. In the Kiwanis Delaware County Tournament, Glen-Nor beat Radnor in the first round, 32-18. In the second round, they overcame Eddystone 24-21 to advance to the semifinals against Prospect Park. Unfortunately, they lost a 25-24 thriller to a last-second shot and were eliminated from advancing to the finals. Edison had to be happy with how his team played late in the season.

On April 9, 1934, Lebanon Valley College announced that Emerson Metoxen had been selected their Director of Athletics. He was chosen from "...a host of candidates that had been narrowed down to ten during the last week." His successes at coaching at the high school and prep school level earned him this promotion. LVC had a history of hiring former Indian School athletes for coaches. In addition being the Athletic Director, the 12-letter alum was hired to coach basketball and baseball and to assist the football coaching.

Emerson spoke at community groups even more than he had done before. He was in demand in part because of his unique background.

The football team went 3-4-1 under new head coach Jerome W. Frock and Emerson as line coach. Emerson's 1934-35 basketball team had worse results, finishing 3 and nine. His baseball team fared a little better, posting a 6-5 season.

The 1935 football team improved dramatically over the previous year, going 6-4-0. The final win was over the Tampa University Spartans at Tampa, Florida in LVC's first intersectional game. The 1935-36 basketball team did worse than the previous year, 3-13. The baseball team again did well going 9-3-1, including 5-1 in league play and one loss and one tie to semipro teams.

The underweight 1936 football team went 3-5. The 1936-37 basketball team went .500 overall and in league. The baseball team didn't do as well, winning only four and losing six. Overall, it wasn't a good year for LVC athletics.

The 1937 football team improved somewhat, going 4-4. The 1937–38 basketball team finished 10-4 for one of the school's most successful seasons in the school's history. The mediocre baseball team compiled a 3-6 season but were .500 in league games.

In 1938, Head Football Coach Jerome W. Frock was promoted to Athletic Director and Emerson was demoted to Assistant Athletic Director. He was released from assisting with the football team but still coached basketball and baseball. At 6-2 the football team had one of its best years in history by scheduling more its size. Scheduling larger schools had brought in more revenue for LVC along with the defeats. The 1938-39 basketball team played better than its 6-9 record indicated because several of its losses were by close scores. Emerson's last baseball team at LVC posted a meager 2-6 record, in part due to having an all-freshman infield. He resigned at the end of the 1939 season.

Emerson next worked for Bethlehem Steel in its physical education department. His name only appeared in print for coaching their basketball team in the YMCA Industrial League. He was still working there when he registered for the WWII draft. In a likely attempt to appear younger and fit for military duty, he shaved a year off his age, claiming to have been born in 1900 instead of 1899.

He started a 22-year tenure at Radnor Junior High School in 1943. He served as athletic director and coached various sports, head coach of some, assistant for others, at both Radnor High School and the junior high. In the mid1950s, his son Martin "Marty" excelled at athletics at Radnor. In 1965 at age 65, their mandatory retirement age, he retired from Radford. The school honored him by creating the Emerson "Chief" Metoxen Spirit Award.

He may have been retired, but he wasn't put on the scrap heap. That summer, he directed Valley Forge Military Academy's Indian Camp. In the fall he became Athletic Director for Eastern Baptist College. He also continued giving talks to community groups as he had been doing for decades.

In 1976, Emerson was enshrined in the Lebanon Valley College Athletic Hall of Fame as one of the six inaugural members. In the 1980s he relocated to Sun City, Arizona, where he died on May 25, 1989 at 90 years of age. He was survived by his wife, three sons, a daughter, and a sister. He was buried at St. David's Church in Radnor Township, Pennsylvania.

James Metoxen

James Metoxen's parentage was unclear. When he enrolled at Carlisle on August 26, 1899, his parents were listed as dead. His home address was Albert Metoxen in Sagola, Wisconsin. It was common to use parents or close relatives for this purpose but, since his parents were both dead, Albert couldn't have been his father. James first shows up on the 1900 Oneida roll as the 16-year-old son of Albert and Celicia Metoxen. Since Celicia would have only been 12 when she had him and her next oldest child was a 4-year-old daughter, it doesn't seem likely that she was his mother. Also, Albert and Celicia were very much alive. Most likely is that Albert and Cecilia opened their home to him after he was orphaned. Later rolls carried him as being born in 1884 as the 1900 one implied. His marriage record, filled out in 1903, listed Simon W.

Name:	James George Metoxen	Nickname:	
DOB:	4/1/1884	Height:	5'9"
Weight:	140 lbs.	Age:	19
Parents:	Simon W. Metoxen Ida Skenandore Metoxen	Home:	Sagola, WI
Early Schooling:	Thomas Indian School		
Later Schooling:			

Metoxen as his father and Ida Skenandore Metoxen as his mother. They were his parents most likely.

He entered Carlisle at the 5th grade, having had 30 months of school previous to this. It is likely that schooling was at Thomas Indian School because he was an orphan. Each summer starting with 1900, he went on an outing to work on a farm. Other than that, little is known about what he did at Carlisle during this enrollment.

James received no mention in the school newspaper until he won the mile run in the 1902 Annual Inter-Class Track and Field meet. He was next heard from in the March 1903 indoor meet for candidates vying to make the school team. He came in second in both the mile and two-mile runs in the 1903 Inter-Class meet. He finished first in the mile run in the dual meet with Bucknell. "Hummingbird and Metoxen could have made better marks in the mile and two-mile run but they were not pushed and Carlisle won all the points in these events easily."

At the State college dual meet, Metoxen won the one-mile run easily, but he accidentally interfered with one of the State College runners and was disqualified by the officials. He apparently didn't compete in the 1904 track meets. After an 11-day-outing completed his enrollment, he went home for the remainder of the summer.

James returned for a second five-year enrollment on August 13, 1904. This time he joined the varsity football team. He may have previously played on a shop team but little was recorded about them. The school newspaper mentioned nothing about his football playing but Second and Third Team (sometimes called Scrubs) games got little press. However, he was included in two different team photos that were printed in newspapers.

In the spring of 1905, he tried out for three track events: ½ mile, 1 mile, and 2 mile. He made the team but didn't win or come in second at any meet.

One Sunday in April, the coal supply for the boiler ran short of coal. James and seven other boys volunteered to do "...the dirty work of hauling coal for the night needs." His name did not appear again in a Carlisle Indian School publication. The only thing in his student records after that was his going on outing to S. H. King in Edgely, Bucks County, Pennsylvania.

In 1910, James was working as a hired man on Edwin Johnson's farm in Upper Makefield Township, Bucks County, Pennsylvania. This would have been a familiar location for him because most of his outings had been in that part of the state.

In 1915 he married Mary Clarkson Philhower in New Jersey. When he registered for the WWI draft in 1917, they were living in Woodside in Bucks County working on a farm owned by William P. Yardley. He listed his DOB as April 1, 1888, possibly to appear younger and more able to fight.

In 1920, he lived in Lower Makefield Township with his wife, Mary E. Metoxen and stepdaughter Mary J Philhower, age 19. The census taker classified them as Black not Indian.

In 1923, James, who was living on Mill Street in Morrisville, Pennsylvania, was sentenced to 30 days in the Bucks County jail. His crime was for throwing his wife against a stove so hard it turned over. He then picked her up bodily and threw her out of the house. She must not have divorced him because the next census listed them as married.

In 1930 they were living on a farm in Newtown Township where he worked. The census taker classified both of them as white this time.

In 1940 they lived and worked on a farm on Lindenhurst Road in Newtown Township. Again, they were classified as white.

He again claimed he was born on April 1, 1888 on his 1942 WWII draft registration. They were then living on Lindenhurst Road, RD 1, Yardley, Bucks County, Pennsylvania.

In 1948, Emerson purchased a lot in Newtown Township from Mabel R. Briggs.

In 1952 he was working for Kauffman Brothers grading Township roads. In December he filed for Social Security benefits, claiming April 1, 1884 as his date of birth.

He died on May 4, 1956 at home in Yardley, Pennsylvania.

Jonas Metoxen

Jonas first arrived at Carlisle on June 28, 1891. The 1885 census, the earliest found that recorded him or his father, listed Jonas as having an older brother, Adam, and sister, Susan. However, he may have had other siblings who, as adults, were no longer listed with their parents. Other Metoxens at Carlisle may well have been his cousins. He surely found a number of other familiar faces given the number of Oneida children there.

After nine months at the school, Jonas began going on outings in the spring that lasted until mid-September. Each year he returned just in time for the start of football season. After Pratt relented on his ban against playing football against other schools in 1893, the newly assembled team played an abbreviated schedule of three games. He was on that squad. In 1894 Carlisle began to play football at the college level in earnest. He played fullback on that team and would not relinquish his

Name: Jonas Abraham Metoxen
Nickname: Man-afraid-of-his-wife
DOB: 3/23/1874
Height: 5'9½"
Weight: 187 lbs.
Age: 24
Parents: Abraham Metoxen
Genisha Nimham Metoxen
Home: Green Bay, WI
Early Schooling: Unknown
Later Schooling:

position for some time. The Carlisle Indians recorded but a single victory in 1894 while their fullback labored in obscurity. That didn't last for long. In 1895, Carlisle played Yale for the first time and Jonas got positive press for his efforts. *The New York World* observed, "The Indians repeatedly worked in wedge on centre, and every time it netted five yards. Occasionally Metoxen got fifteen and twenty." In the last game of the season, he injured his knee while running back a kickoff against the New York City Y. M. C. A. team, a team that was bolstered by several members of the Crescent Athletic Club. *The World* reporter opined that the Indians would have scored three more touchdowns had it not been for Referee Underwood: "Those Indians will go away with a poor idea of Christianity if that robbery keeps up," growled Harry Stevens. "Talk about your hold ups!" He went on to say, "When Metoxen was carried off the field with a wrenched knee he surprised everybody by blubbering with pain. So much for the inherent stoicism of the race."

Just before the 1896 season, columnist Owen Langdon commented on the team's prospects and appearance:

> "The Indians are remarkably good players, everything considered. One of their best men last year, Pierce, a fine guard and worthy of a great Varsity team, has very pronounced Indian features. Metoxen, the fullback, Wheelock, the left guard, and others of the team were less pronouncedly Indian in appearance. The team as a whole was decidedly good and will probably be no worse this year."

In the infamous Yale game in which the Indians were robbed of a touchdown and a victory, former Yale star Harry Beecher discussed the game for *The World*. He described the Indian ball carriers' work on what should have been the decisive drive: "Seneca, Metoxen, and Pierce made decisive gains, and seemingly had no trouble in fooling with the Blue's rush line. They ran, crawled and rolled ahead, always with the ball." The November 6 *New York Times* commented on an editorial titled, "What is important is that the Carlisle football team of 1896 has given no irrefragable proof of the ennobling power of education on the Indian," from what the *Times* called "an interesting neighbor of ours." The *Times* went on to say that the article was intended,

"...to be complimentary to METOXEN, LONE WOLF, and the other red gladiators of the gridiron." From this one can conclude that the eastern newspapers considered Jonas Metoxen to be one of Carlisle's star players.

The game after the Yale game, the one with Harvard, was so important the University of Michigan student newspaper, the *Michigan Daily*, sent a reporter to cover it. Its reporter observed, "...Metoxen, with the longest, blackest kind of football hair, throwing a Harvard halfback right over his head. It was a perfectly clean game, no slugging, but four Harvard men had to quit because they ran their heads too hard against the Indian line, which might just as well have been made of brick."

After the game the following week with Penn, *The Atlanta Constitution* ran an article titled, "A Scalp for Pennsy," and subtitled, "Mighty Metoxen Powerless: Great Indian Full-Back Plunged Uselessly Into the Line." A section of the article contradicted that a bit:

Metoxen's Great Playing

"Two plunges and Metoxen and H. Pierce carried the ball to Pennsylvania's ten-yard line. Cayou went around the left end for five yards. Then he went around the right end and was thrown by Overfield two yards from the coveted chalk line. It was the first down, and it looked as if nothing could save a touchdown. From thousands of Pennsylvanians' throats came the appealing cry, 'Hold them, Pen.'

"Straight into the mass of men Metoxen plunged. The line held, but none could tell if beneath that mass of men the Indian back had gone over for a touchdown. A wild shout rent the air when the players were pulled off each other and Metoxen was seen lying with the ball on but not over the goal line.

"There were still two downs, and one Inch, to gain. Not a sound arose from 15,000 people as the men lined up. It was a grim grapple, and not one of those twenty-two men but would have broken a limb or even his neck to make or save the touchdown. The Quakers crouched close to the ground like so many wild beasts waiting to spring. With clenched teeth and fierce faces the Indians hurled themselves upon their foes. There was an awful crush and swaying of fighting men, and the great human mass went down in a heap together.

"Again came that dead silence as the men sullenly rolled off each other in response to the referee's whistle. Then again that triumphant shout arose, for the white men had met the onslaught and Metoxen had again been stopped right on the line. One more chance remained. As Metoxen dashed into the line the Quaker rushers heaved forward and threw the entire Indian team back, and the touchdown was lost by six inches. Then the referee's whistle blew and the game was over."

When interviewed before the Thanksgiving Day game with Brown, Metoxen commented on the Indians' play against Penn:

"It has been our custom when about to take part in a big game to sleep the night previous in the town where the game is to be played. This resulted in giving our team plenty of rest. We didn't follow the plan this time, however, but remained in Carlisle overnight. Then, in order to make time, we were called very early in the morning, ate our breakfast at 5 o'clock, and took the train for Philadelphia. Rising so early and traveling several hours in the train tired the boys very much, and they were quite listless when they went on Franklin Field."

Due to an injury in the game with Cincinnati, Jonas did not start the game with Brown. But it became necessary for him to play when, early in the second half, McFarland was injured. He was ineffective when playing hurt. Although Carlisle lost to each of The Big Four in successive weeks and to Brown on Thanksgiving Day, the 5-5 season was considered a success because it included thumpings of Penn State, Cincinnati, and Duquesne plus a decisive win over Wisconsin, that year's Champions of the West, under the lights in the Chicago Coliseum. Jonas starred against Wisconsin and there was a humorous sidelight to the game. Two of Bemus Pierce's kickoffs hit the iron arches that supported the Coliseum's roof. By playing the toughest possible opposition, and on the road, Carlisle was developing a reputation as were its stars. A wire-service article printed across the country featured a full-length drawing plus a write up:

AN INDIAN FULL BACK
Jonas Metoxen, a Pillar of Strength to the Carlisle Football Team

"One of the best men on the famous Carlisle Indian school football team is Jonas Metoxen, the full back. His name in its original form was Met-the-Oxen, but in the process of civilization the included article 'the' was assimilated and the decidedly Christian title Jonas was prefixed. But 'the play's the thing,' and the play of Jonas is of a kind that gives it rank with that of the best on any gridiron. Metoxen is an Oneida Indian. He stands 5 feet 9½ inches high and weighs 187 pounds. The strongest feature of his work is line bucking, and in this he is admittedly excellent, and many of the best scores made by the Indians during the season have been directly traceable to the strong plays of Metoxen."

In March 1897, the following item circulated around the country:

"The Carlisle Indian football team will be greatly weakened next year by the loss of many of the best players. Metoxen goes to Princeton, Lone Wolf and Cayou to Chicago University, and two more of the players to Wisconsin."

Lone Wolf returned to Oklahoma, however Cayou and Metoxen remained at their usual positions for the upcoming season, although Cayou wasn't expected to play because of injuries. He later went to the University of Illinois.

JONAS METOXEN.

The 1897 version of the Carlisle Indian team continued to show improvement, especially in the kicking game, but still included losses to the Big Four teams they played that year. Before the season started, *The New York World* depicted Jonas falling on a loose ball. After the game with Penn, the *Record* observed, "Metoxen—he's harder to stop than a whole team of oxen." Jonas's punting improved to the point that he was considered better than any man Yale could put up against him. The team had a winning season but lost to the three Big Four teams they played plus Brown.

In the spring of 1898, Joseph Metoxen, Jonas's uncle, announced that the Wisconsin Oneidas had formed two companies of soldiers to fight in the war against Spain. Neither company had officers because they preferred to be led by "...army or militia officers, who understand white man's style of fighting." The would-be soldiers practiced drilling on the reservation under the direction of several war veterans well past the age limit for enlistees. They also organized a band that was to accompany the troops. One supposes that a Wheelock was involved with the band. The elder Metoxen reported that his nephew wrote him from Carlisle to inform him that his classmates were ready to organize a company to fight in Cuba. Joseph also said that he attempted to form, as he expressed it, "plenty big Injun army" that would have included soldiers from the Menominee and Stockbridge reservations as well as some from Brothertown on Lake Winnebago. It appears that his attempts failed.

That October, Jonas scored a touchdown in an early-season loss to Cornell, but the Indians' play impressed their opponents' coach, Glenn S. "Pop" Warner. The 1898 team posted another winning record but

Jonas Metoxen at Carlisle

yet again a victory over even one of the Big Four eluded them. After the season ended, Jonas returned home as his enrollment had ended. But he didn't just lie about. In the summer, he played for the Oneida team against Green Bay at the annual Oneida Fair.

For years pundits had declared that all the Carlisle Indians needed to become a championship team was a good coach. In 1899, Superintendent Pratt finally hired one. After Pop Warner took the helm, the Indians never looked back. However, Jonas wasn't there; he was back home playing for the local Wisconsin National Guard team, Marinette Company I. Exactly why Jonas returned to Carlisle on October 18 is unclear. It may have been that several Indians were injured early in the season and he felt they needed his help. Or, Warner may have asked him to return. It took Jonas awhile to learn Warner's new signals and his new position at right halfback. Shuffling players in response to injuries incurred in the loss to Princeton on November 11, Warner shifted the badly bruised Metoxen back to his old position at fullback for the game with Oberlin. That was a good move because he proved to be a human battering ram against the hapless Oberlin line and left the game at half time due to having run up an insurmountable lead. Jonas closed out the regular season by routinely plunging through the Columbia line for 10 yards at a clip. That victory earned the Indians a trip to San Francisco where the Indians defeated the University of California on Christmas Day. This game made the Indians the first team to play games on both coasts. On the way back, Jonas and his teammates played the mismatched Phoenix Indian School team to complete the school's best year to that time. Jonas closed out his Carlisle career with a 9-2 season that included Carlisle's first win over a Big Four team, Penn. Metoxen returned home shortly after the season ended.

Before the post-season games were played, sports writers announced that Jonas would be entering Lawrence University in the fall and would be trying out for the football team. He selected Lawrence, located in Appleton, Wisconsin, because of its close proximity to his home. But when fall came, he played for the Marinette team.

The announcement of Jonas's upcoming marriage provided the reason for the switch. His bride was Phoebe Baird (Ya-go-win in Oneida), a former student of both Carlisle and Hampton Institute.

FOOTBALL TEAM OF 1900

They married on November 11, 1900 in the Hobart Episcopal mission church. Wedding guests included the Honorable Isaac Stephenson, a wealthy lumberman and early Progressive politician, as well as the officers and members of Company I of Marinette. Stephenson presented a beautiful set of silverware as a wedding gift from the group.

Jonas's name didn't disappear from the sports pages as he continued to play football on the local Marinette team and someone named a racehorse Metoxen, presumably in his honor. However, not everyone noticed. As early as January 1902, an unattributed newspaper column reported on his absence from the pages of the national press: "James [sic] Metoxen, the Indian who a few years ago was the star player on the Carlisle football team and received many ovations from patrons of the sport and much notice from eastern newspaper scribes is now living in semi-obscurity in the little village of Preble." His obscurity was broken by a November 1902 newspaper article that stated the Marinette team lost a game to South Bend because Metoxen didn't play. According to the reporter, Jonas's wife wouldn't let him. That led to locals dubbing him "Man-Afraid-of-His-Wife."

A February 1904 wire service article titled "Metoxen, Fullback, Now Works on Farm" told of Jonas's life on the farm cutting cordwood in winter and driving a team (of horses or mules) to deliver it to a paper mill in Appleton, Wisconsin. It also mentioned he had found a way to get involved with a local football team each fall. When interviewed, he seemed more pleased with the results of his labor than from any government largess: "We get a few cents from the Government for Christmas, but that's all." He picked up a silk-lined overcoat from the seat next to him and said: "That's what I used to get when I played football, and now, umph, get darn little." The reporter opined: "With the reputation this man had he could easily be demanding a comfortable salary from some big university as a coach, had not his native instincts been so strong that as soon as he was out of college he went back to his former haunts on the reservation." When contacted about this, Superintendent Pratt pointed out that not one of the football players had drifted back to idleness although some had not done as well as Jonas, who was saving up to buy more land.

By 1910, Jonas and Phoebe's family had grown to include sons Elmer and Irvin along with daughters Eunice, Josephine, and Helen. Soon, daughters Nellie, Birdena, and Alice were added to the brood. In 1910, Superintendent Friedman wrote to former football players to inquire about how they were doing and requested photographs. Jonas sent him one of his farmhouse. The next year, he submitted a Record of Graduates and Returned Students. Metoxen hadn't taken further schooling after leaving Carlisle and he had married Phoebe Baird. He described their home as a three-bedroom, two-story frame house he built shortly after they were married. The farm consisted of 82 acres of land on which were stables and a granary. He planned to build a barn the following spring. His livestock consisted of three horses, 5 cows, and a calf. Jonas had never worked for the Indian Service but had worked off the farm one winter as a blacksmith.

In 1914, Jimmy Callahan, manager of the Chicago White Sox, told of an experience he had two years prior to that:

> "With several others I left Camp Jerome, [owner Charles] Comiskey's camp, on a long tramp after a world's championship games two years ago. Our course

took us through the clearing which skirted Little Bass Lake in Wisconsin. We went through the swamp land across the Flambeau River and then around Turtle Lake. That was some walk and took us through some wild country. Jogging along—and talking in a loud voice, which is excellent when hunting—we came to the edge of a small birch forest and into a dense thicket. Turning at an abrupt bend, we almost ran into an Indian in tattered trousers, ancient Mackinaw coat, and leather leggings. He was taken by complete surprise. The Indian grinned a greeting of 'Howdy,' and to our astonishment, asked: 'Say, can you tell me who won the world's series?' That man was Metoxen, one of the greatest football and baseball players ever turned out of Carlisle."

In 1917, as the U. S. entered WWI, Jonas attempted to organize an Oneida troop to be part of an Indian regiment from Wisconsin. The War Department did not form Indian regiments but integrated the 13,000 Indians who enlisted into existing units.

By 1930, Jonas and Phoebe had moved off the farm and into Menasha, Wisconsin where he worked at a paper mill. A local newspaper article with an accompanying photograph informed residents of his exploits on the gridiron after an old fan recognized him and told the newspaper about Metoxen. Jonas related a humorous story about an incident that occurred in a game he played in against a local team in Wisconsin after he left Carlisle. A Menasha man on the opposing team was carrying the ball when he saw Jonas bearing down on him. Rather than letting Jonas tackle him, he simply tossed him the ball.

Phoebe died in February 1934 at about 55 years of age and was buried at Oneida after the funeral at St. Thomas Episcopal Church in Menasha. The cause of her death wasn't stated. The 1937 census listed Emily Doxtator as Jonas's second wife. According to an April 1939 newspaper article, Jonas and Mamie King filed for a marriage license. The January 1939 Tomah Agency roll listed Emily Doxtator King Metoxen as married and George King as divorced. Mamie might have been Emily's nickname and they must have put off getting a church wedding for a few years.

Jonas was injured seriously in an automobile accident in September 1939. He had 6 broken ribs and a broken left leg. His wife, Emily or Mamie—one assumes because her first name wasn't included in the newspaper account—had her right leg broken in addition to some other unspecified injuries. His son, Irving Metoxen, the driver of the car in which Jonas was riding, pled guilty to drunken driving and was fined $100 plus costs or 90 days in the county jail. His driver's license was revoked as he had a history of public drunkenness. Jonas's other son, Elmer, was also in the car and was fined $10 and costs or 15 days in Winnebago County jail. Both took the jail sentences. Mr. and Mrs. Metoxen were both treated at St. Elizabeth's Hospital in Menasha. She was released shortly after treatment, but he was in the hospital for about three weeks. A 1940 insurance settlement with the Hardware Mutual Casualty Company gave Jonas $2,000, Mrs. Metoxen $100, and Elmer $250, one assumes, for their injuries.

On July 18, 1942, Jonas Metoxen drowned in the Fox River Canal in Menasha. He and his wife were walking along the canal wall when he lost his footing and fell in. He was believed to be 68 years old at the time.

Job J. Moore

Job Jacob Moore arrived at Carlisle on August 19, 1899 at age 16. Unfortunately, his student file included little more than a listing of his outings, that he was trained as a blacksmith, and a newspaper clipping that turned out to be incorrect. Even his parentage was unclear. His father's name and he was likely Stockbridge were about the only things known about him. Fortunately, finding a marriage license cleared up much of it.

Job had some prior schooling, most likely at Thomas Indian School. That allowed him to enter Carlisle in the second grade. It was later learned he was born in Chilton, Wisconsin near the Stockbridge Reservation. His Oneida heritage may have been through his mother.

He almost immediately went on outing to J. Satterthwaite in Trenton, New Jersey. If his student record was correct, Job spent most of his

Name:	Job J. Moore	Nickname:	
DOB:	4/1/1884	Height:	5'11"
Weight:	152 lbs.	Age:	16
Parents:	Jacob Moore Hattie Cornelius Moore	Home:	Sagola, WI
Early Schooling:	Thomas Indian School		
Later Schooling:			

first four years on outing, returning to Carlisle in time for the start of the 1903-04 school year and football season.

Moore received no mention in school publications but a few newspaper articles attested to him having played on the 1903 Carlisle football team. He played left tackle for the Carlisle Reserves against the Harrisburg Students on October 10, 1903. Job's play must have impressed the coaches because he got moved up to the varsity squad as a substitute. He got playing time at left tackle in the varsity's 6–6 tie of Virginia on November 22, 1903 and in the varsity's 28–0 defeat of Northwestern on November 26. His playing in both of these games meant he had been elevated to the traveling squad. It isn't known if he went with the team to California for the post-season games because his name wasn't listed in the line-ups.

Job completed his five-year term of enrollment in the sixth grade. Since he was on outings so much of his time at Carlisle, he must have been attending the public schools at the outing sites. He left for home on June 25, 1904 and set about farming his land and blacksmithing on the side. He married Julia Cornelius, daughter of Elias and Celicia Cornelius, on December 25, 1904. She had some education, probably at Oneida Boarding school.

Their child, Florence, was born on January 15, 1907. Her birth certificate listed her as male but all subsequent records are female. That her birth wasn't recorded until May 20 and by a clerk who was not present at her birth may account for the error.

Cynthia Webster Moore

Julia died on February 25, 1907 of septicemia, sometimes called maternal sepsis, leaving Job a widower with an infant to care for and raise. He married Cynthia Webster on August 2 that year. As an old-maid schoolteacher at 32 years of age, she surely took taking on this responsibility with trepidation. She had spent five years at Carlisle Indian School, the last two and a half enrolled at

Carlisle High School, graduating in 1898. She left Carlisle in August 1898 to begin a career of teaching in the Indian Service at Pottawatomie, Kansas. By 1907, she had taught at four different schools. That summer she was working at Oneida Boarding school as a substitute baker. The proximity to Job's farm to the school may have made each aware of the other. Taking on the responsibilities of being both a farm wife and mother to an infant at the same time would have been daunting enough without her previous experience weighing on her.

A year earlier, Cynthia was set to be married to James W. Silas, a railroad fireman who had graduated from Haskell Institute in Lawrence, Kansas. All the preparations had been made and the invitations had been sent out. But some days before the wedding,

> "[T]he groom sent word to his father that he would not be at the wedding and that they would never see him again. He gave no reason for his sudden change of mind. Search was made for him by his relatives, but he had disappeared...[D]eserting his bride at the eleventh hour is the sensation of the year on the reservation."

This time, the groom had reasons not to skip out. Nothing is known about the ceremony except that it took place. The 1910 census suggested that the marriage was a success because they had added two children of their own to the family: Charles, almost two, and Mildred, four months. They owned and worked their own farm but it had a mortgage.

In January 1911, he wrote Superintendent Moses Friedman requesting help in getting employment in the Indian Service. After investigating Job, who had left Carlisle long before he arrived, Friedman sent a formal request to Charles Dagenette, Supervisor of Indian Employment and a Carlisle graduate, stating:

> "Job Moore is a blacksmith by trade although he has been farming for the last few years...He is 27 years old and a 'hustler,' very industrious and trustworthy in every way. He also married a graduate, Cynthia Webster, who

has taught for many years in the service. I trust you may be able to help them."

How long it took isn't known but the Moores were at Cross Lake School, Ponemah, Minnesota in January 1913. Job worked as a blacksmith there while Cynthia kept house.

In 1920, they were back living and working on Job's farm. In the interim, Job and Cynthia had three more children: Raymond, Vivian, and Mabel and hadn't lost any of the three older ones.

By 1930 with the Great Depression underway, they had moved to Waukegan, Illinois where they lived in a rented house. Job worked as a blacksmith for a breakwater builder. Cynthia and Florence worked as cooks at a sanatorium. Mildred was a stenographer at an asbestos products company.

In 1940, they lived at 1013 Poplar Street in Waukegan. Neither Job nor Cynthia worked. Florence worked as a domestic where Raymond and Vivian were shop workers, he at a wire mill and she at a building products factory.

In 1950 they lived at 1108 Hickory Street in Waukegan. Raymond was the only child still living at home. He worked for a company specializing in prefabricated construction.

1, Lubo; 2, Dillon; 3, Bowen; 4, Williams; 5, Warner, Coach; 6, Flores; 7, Sheldon; 8, Mathews; 9, Charles; 10, Jude; 11, Johnson; 12, Hendricks; 13, Exendine; 14, White; 15, Shouschuk.
Photo by Choate.
CARLISLE INDIAN SCHOOL.

Job died on April 6, 1956 after a long illness. He had been blind for 18 years. His obituary claimed he had been a teammate of Jim Thorpe at Carlisle. Jim Thorpe didn't arrive until February 6, 1904, after the 1903 football season was over. Job left in June and Jim didn't get involved in Carlisle athletics until 1907. However, Job did play under Pop Warner alongside such stars as James Johnson and Frank Mount Pleasant.

Amos Reed

Amos Read arrived at Carlisle for a five-year enrollment on October 10, 1895 at 22 years of age. His reasons for coming may have been to avoid problems with the law or to start over. He was having a bad year. In January, he had been arrested for bringing alcohol onto the Oneida Nation and was sent to Milwaukee to face a grand jury. The punishment, if there was any, couldn't have lasted too long because he was arrested again in August. This time he was charged for being drunk and disorderly. After he pled guilty, Justice Nys sentenced him to seven days in jail and fined him $7.30.

His sparse student file said nothing about his academic grade level or the outings he went on. He must have had some prior schooling because he could read and write cursive with better-than-legible hand-

Name:	Amos Reed	Nickname:	
DOB:	2/9/1873	Height:	6'
Weight:	162 lbs.	Age:	21
Parents:	John Reed Elizabeth Reed	Home:	Oneida, WI
Early Schooling:	School unknown		
Later Schooling:	None		

writing. School publications made no mention of him while he was there. Amos later wrote about working on the school farm: "I never forget I used to plow the hurn[5] nine o'clock good night when I was at Carlisle."

He came to campus too late to make the varsity line-up in 1895 because football season had already started. A very good athlete, he probably played on the scrubs, likely the Second Team, but they got little to no press at that time. A good pitcher, he probably played on the school's baseball team in the spring until he got into trouble. On May 14, 1896, Judge Biddle found Reed guilty of assault and battery while intoxicated and sentenced him to 120 days in the Carlisle jail, for which he had already served 30. He would have gotten out of jail well ahead of time for the 1896 football season.

Surprisingly, he later wrote that he enjoyed school life very much, especially being in the band and playing on the football and baseball teams. Amos wasn't at Carlisle long enough to make much of a splash the school was willing to publicize. He ran away in May 1897 and never returned. School officials may have advised him to leave for his and the school's best interests.

Back at home, he pitched for the Oneida Nation team but, in August 1898 signed with the Twin Cities club. That same week he struck out 16 batters in a victory over the White Stars team. In November when playing left guard for the Oneida football team, he wrenched his knee in a game against Stevens Point Normal. The newspaper's line-up was less than useful.

The teams lined up as follows:

Oneidas	Position	Stevens Point
Metoxen	center	Cowan
Metoxen	right guard	Soper
Reed	left guard	Sager
Metoxen	right tackle	Karl
Skenadore	left tackle	Nelson
Metoxen	right end	Mathe
Metoxen	left end	Karnopp
Metoxen	right half	Argyle
Smith	left half	Bradford
Parkhurst	quarter	Smith
Skenadore	full	Manz, capt

Umpire and referee, Sylvester and McCaskill; time keeper, Southwick; linesmen, Werner, Hanzlick.

---

[5] a disused part of a field

In 1899 Connie Mack visited the Oneida Nation incognito possibly to check out phenoms Amos Reed and Chauncey Baird. Nothing apparently came of his secret trip. A gossipy article in the December 15 edition of a local newspaper wrote:

> "Amos Reed, the famous baseball pitcher, is aspiring to a nice Christmas present. Rumor is afloat that Miss Katie Metoxen has resigned her position in his favor. We will be able to judge better by next Wednesday."

Katie Metoxen Reed

Katie, also a Carlisle alum, had overlapped with Amos at the school, so they could have gotten to know each other then. After finishing her enrollment at Carlisle, Katie worked as assistant cook at Oneida Boarding School. She married Amos on December 20, 1899 in a ceremony conducted by Rev. W. W. Souler.

The 1900 Federal Census listed him as working as a farmer and retired, presumedly from paid athletics. In 1910 Amos and Katie had a son and three daughters living in their own mortgage-free home. He was working odd jobs and was listed as blind. However, his disability may have been something other than blindness.

Amos wrote Superintendent Friedman in 1911 about his failing health. He then had five children, the oldest being eleven. Katie wrote in 1912 that, in addition to her housework, she made lace for a New York company. Three of her children were attending Oneida Boarding School. Her baby boy was 16 months old and learning to walk. "We think of nothing but him." She also wrote about her surroundings: "I have a nice little home, some apple trees, cherry trees, current plum trees, grapes, and other trees by the house that makes the home so pleasant." She mentioned that the only English words she could speak when she entered Carlisle in 1891 were yes and no.

In 1913 Amos sent a postcard to Friedman on which he wrote that his present occupation was hunting every day. Blindness would have prevented him from doing that, so his disability had to be something else.

His September 12, 1918 WWI draft registration listed his occupation as invalid and described his condition as partly paralyzed.

The 1920 Federal Census listed them as living at 1112 Cedar Street in Green Bay and Katie as working at a meat packing plant.

Amos died on December 14, 1929 following a 20-year period of ill health. He was survived by his wife, four daughters and two sons.

Caleb Sickles

Caleb Mathew Sickles, a 12-year-old Oneida, arrived in Carlisle in August 1891 and enrolled for the standard-at-that-time five-year term. He was 4'6" tall then, but his weight was not recorded. At the end of the summer after graduation in 1898, he re-enrolled for an indeterminate period, listed then as age 21. The enrollment forms that were found included good information, including his father's name, Martin, Caleb was half blood, and he was from the Sagola Agency in Wisconsin. However, much information was missing or unclear. His mother was listed as living, but her name was left blank. Perusing census records and Carlisle Indian School publications led one to conclude that Caleb,

Name:	Caleb Matthew Sickles	Nickname:	Sick
DOB:	12/27/1880	Height:	4'6"
Weight:	138 lbs.	Age:	12
Parents:	Martin Sickles Semantha Titus Sickles	Home:	Little Rapids, WI
Early Schooling:	Oneida Indian School Tomah Indian School		
Later Schooling:	Dickinson College Preparatory School Ohio Medical University		

sometimes misprinted as Carl, was the son of Martin Sickles, a full-blood Oneida, and Smantha or Thimantha but likely Semantha Titus Sickles(her name was spelled differently on each census), a white woman. Caleb was born in Munsey, Ontario (in the English-speaking part of Canada). Semantha was born in Michigan. The rest of their children were born in Wisconsin. The 1910 census listed Semantha as the mother of 13, 12 living, one of whom was Raymond O., who was living with Caleb at that time.

Several other Sickles attended Carlisle but don't appear to have been Caleb's siblings. One newspaper article specifically mentioned that Martha, Florence and Arthur were siblings but omitted any mention of Caleb, something that would have been unlikely, given his celebrity, had he been their sibling. However, the August 26, 1898 issue of *The Indian Helper* casually mentioned Arthur as being Caleb's brother. Superintendent Friedman inquired about Arthur's whereabouts in 1910. From Caleb's response, it would be difficult to determine if they were brothers, cousins or no relation at all. The vagueness of his response may have been due to being overly familiar with the issue.

Home for the Sickles was in central Wisconsin. The Oneida Reservation extends from Green Bay to Outagamie County, the next county over. While some Oneidas lived within the Green Bay city limits, Martin Sickles was listed on the various censuses as being a farmer in Outagamie County. In 1898, Dickinson College listed Caleb's home as Little Rapids, Wisconsin. Later Caleb wrote, "I have never lived among the Indians to any extent." He may have meant that he had been at boarding schools since an early age as were many of his peers or that his family, although listed as Oneida, lived 5 miles from the reservation at Little Rapids. Thus, Caleb did not have an on-reservation childhood, and attending Carlisle probably required less adjustment on his part than it would have required from many of his classmates.

Caleb received his first newspaper coverage in the November 15, 1895 edition of *The Indian Helper* in an article that stated, "Misses Ely and Burgess, and Masters Johnnie Given, Caleb Stickles, George Conners, and Ernest Peters went by wheel to Mechanicsburg late Saturday afternoon, returning in the deep shadow of the evening." Apparently he had taken up cycling, which was all the rage at that time. It's not clear whether the Misses, Carlisle faculty members, chaperoned the boys or whether the boys went along as protectors. On modern roads, assuming a time when there is little traffic, and on modern bi-

Caleb Sickles with his mother

cycles, that 10-mile ride would be a breeze, as long as one didn't get run over by the cars. However, in pre-automobile times, Trindle Road, the most direct route between Carlisle and Mechanicsburg, was a a rural dirt road full of hazards.

Caleb started to work in the print shop after the holidays, according to *The Indian Helper*. He continued there for some years and became a valuable worker. By April of that year, 1896, Caleb had joined the Invincible Debating Society. He was given high marks for what was likely his first major public speaking appearance, "Caleb Sickles made a happy hit in a recitation very naturally rendered... " A week later he, James Wheelock, and Albert Nash participated in the entertainment given by the YMCA in town. Unfortunately, the nature of their participation was not mentioned. By this time, 1896, he was allowed to leave the school for the summer, but it is not known whether it was to work somewhere or to return home. Most likely it was to work at a paying job because, in later summers, he earned money working at the New Jersey shore. After returning to school and the print shop, Caleb, now a Junior, was elected secretary of the Invincibles.

John S. Steckbeck, in *Fabulous Redmen,* lists Sickles as playing on the varsity football team in 1897 and 1898. Game reports make no mention of him and don't include his name in the lineups. He was most likely a substitute, no mean feat on teams that included the likes of Ed Rogers, Frank Cayou, the Pierce brothers, Frank Hudson, Jonas

Metoxen, and Martin Wheelock. This was just the start, not the end, of his football career.

Caleb graduated from Carlisle in the spring of 1898 and enrolled in the Dickinson College Preparatory School at age 21. Dickinson College's first game of the season—promising prep school players were allowed to dress for varsity games—was on September 24 against Susquehanna University. Caleb's name was not in the lineup, but a Mr. Sickles of the Indian School umpired the game. In mid-October he got into a game. He played quarterback for the Dickinson College Prep School team in a game against Harrisburg High School and got press clippings for doing "the best work." The next game, a scoreless tie with nearby Shippensburg Normal School, found him at left end, the position he would play the rest of the year. He carried the ball a lot in Prep's offensive scheme and consistently made good yardage. He became a star at the prep school.

After football season ended, Caleb went out for Prep's basketball team and was a starter at one of the attack (known as forward today) positions. In the spring of 1899 he competed in a track meet with Mercersburg Academy and Franklin and Marshall College, coming in second in the 12-yard special event and third in the special open 120-yard dash. His best event that day was the relay race, the first and arguably most exciting, event. *The Dickinsonian* gushed:

> "... But when the crowd saw young Sickles of Dickinson take his place at the line and wait on tiptoes to touch the hand of his panting colleague, and then dash off on the last lap with an astonishingly increasing speed, the chances for our Preps, because suddenly bright, but the distance was too great to be made up, and Mercersburg came in first, although their lead was quite perceptively decreased by Sickles who was heartily cheered."

In May, he played left field and pitched for the Indian School baseball team in a game against Dickinson College and lost 3-2. His relief pitching may have been the difference that day as he walked three batters and committed a balk. However, the reporter thought he had the potential to become a good left-handed pitcher.

In July *The Indian Helper* shared Caleb's note from his summer job, calling it a "friendly letter." The article reported:

> "At the Beacon by the Sea [in Point Pleasant], New Jersey, a number of our boys are spending their summer waiting on table, and doing other work demanded of them. The other day they played a game of ball with the Trenton Military Academy and won by the score of 21 to 3. Siceni Nori, '94 who is living near Trenton, pitched for the Academy team."

October of 1899 found Pop Warner coaching the Carlisle Indian School football team for the first time. Caleb was still at the Dickinson College Preparatory School but played right end for Carlisle as a substitute for Joseph Scholder. His moment in the limelight came when he played the entire game in Carlisle's big win over Penn, their first ever against one of the Big Four.

Sickles completed his education at Prep in the spring and left for summer employment, first in Philadelphia, then on the Jersey Shore. In July 1900, *The Indian Helper* reprinted an article from a Point Pleasant newspaper, *The Beacon,* about the Independence Day races held as part of their festivities:

> "The running of Sickles, the Carlisle student, was the chief feature of the foot races. At the tape he won by a few inches. Sickles is such a clean, good fellow that he deserves all he won, and the crowd was with him, and the red man's praise became the 'white man's burden' at the end of each race."

A month later, *The Red Man and Helper* reported,

> "Caleb Sickles, '99, spent Sunday with us on his way to Columbus, Ohio, where he intends to work his way through Medical College. Caleb has been spending a part of the summer working at the seashore. He looks in splendid condition, and has kept himself under athletic training. He intends that his athletics shall play no small part in getting him his M. D. diploma. The name

of Dr. Sickles already runs through the ears of the Man-on-the-bandstand, and we desire him to realize his highest hopes."

Pratt was not the only one pleased to see one of his students strive for professional education. Whether Caleb changed his mind or the newspaper got it wrong is unclear, an M. D. diploma was not in his future. Other opportunities awaited him instead.

At the end of the 1901 season, the *Ohio State Journal* published a large write-up titled, "Good for the Indian Captain," that celebrated Caleb's election as captain of the Ohio Medical University football team for 1902. He was described as being 21 years of age [likely wrong] and a junior in the Dental Department. Either he changed majors or Miss Burgess, his former supervisor in the printing department, had had it wrong earlier. When writing about Sickles' play, the *Journal* reporter wrote, "In his time he has gained the reputation of being one of the best, if not the very best end in Ohio. He is a hard and sure tackler, as well as very fast in the interference and a sure man when called upon to advance the ball." Dr. W. J. Means of the Athletic Board was quoted as saying, "The choice of Sickles for Captain is very satisfactory to me. We always like men who are well up in their classes as our athletic leaders, and Sickles, in addition to his football ability, is one of the best students in the university."

In April 1903, *The Red Man and Helper* reported,

> "Mr. Caleb Sickles '98, a student of the Ohio Medical College, Columbus, Ohio, is with us for a brief visit. He is taking a course in dentistry and hopes to finish in another year. This spring and summer he will earn some wherewithal on the New York State Baseball League, and is now on his way to Syracuse. Caleb had pneumonia a year ago and does not look as robust as before he was taken ill, but says he is feeling well now. He intends starting out in business for himself as soon as he finishes. Sickles, Sickles, Sickles! Rah! Rah! Rah!"

Superintendent Pratt could hardly constrain his enthusiasm. Or was it Marianna Burgess? It was not always clear. In its next issue, *The Red Man and Helper* wrote, "Dr. Caleb Sickles has gone to Syracuse, where, as was stated last week, he will play ball on the N. Y. League, this season. He says dental Seniors in the Columbus University are called Doctors, and we wish to be one of the first to give him the well-earned title."

A May 8 article shared some bad news: "...finding that his injured arm did not permit him to play ball as actively as the League requires... He will get employment in Columbus for the summer and finish his Dental course next year." A week later he was negotiating with the Portsmouth, Ohio team. In June he was playing left field for the Lancaster, Ohio club.

Caleb Sickles ably captained the 1903 Ohio Medical University football team and, in October, was called on to help his former O. M. U. coach, John Eckstorm, prepare the Kenyon College team for their big game with Ohio State. At the end of the school year, Sickles graduated from dental school. In late May or very early June 1904, Caleb wrote Miss Burgess:

> "It has been some time since you have heard from me. I am through school now and am in the employ of the State. I have a position here at the State hospital. I have been here over three weeks. The day I graduated I was about "broke" but since, I have been getting a few dollars together, and am on my feet again, as it were. I am drawing pay here as an attendant on a good Ward, and doing the dental work-for the employees and some of the patients; combining the two I make quite a little sum. I have also had the good fortune to be selected to coach for Heidelberg University at Tin, Ohio. They have quite a school there. While the position does not pay so very much compared with salaries that some coaches get, yet it will be a great help to me this fall. I will get $275 and all expenses for my services for nine weeks. I can never make $275 any easier. They want me to be Athletic Director the year round at a salary of $700. The town is a good one and I have a chance to locate there permanently. I think it would be a good thing for me to accept, but I want to locate in the West and grow up with the town.

"One thing I am glad of, that is I have lost interest in playing baseball and football. I play here every Saturday for the Hospital, that's how I came to get my position. I have a good many privileges with it. Business has been rather brisk with me for the past few days. The other day I made $7.50, and yesterday I made four. Friday I'll make four more, besides my pay as an attendant goes on every day and I am getting all my expenses too. By the time fall comes around I'll have a little money."

His change of heart regarding playing the games must have been very recent as just a month earlier *The Newark Daily Advocate* published an article about his baseball playing:

"Caleb Sickles, the full-blooded Indian who played several time in Newark last season, is now covering center field for Manager James' Unions. The fleet-footed red man gave an exhibition of the speed that has made him famous on two occasions Sunday. In the sixth he dumped a slow one down the third base foul line which Snyder quickly gathered in and made a perfect throw to Francis, but Sickles had already crossed the bag. Again in the eighth, Sickles nearly beat out an infield hit, many believing he got to first ahead of Durch's beautiful throw, but Richards called him out."

Apparently, after acquiring gainful employment and a coaching job, he lost interest in getting bumps and bruises as a player. Or, knowing the disdain schools had for their coaches playing professionally, he may have spoken preemptorily.

The October 13, 1904 issue of *The Arrow* shared that Joel Cornelius was then in Tiffin, Ohio with Caleb Sickles. He was taking a business course at Heidelberg University and, of course, playing football. Like many others from Carlisle, Caleb gave his former schoolmates opportunities when he had the chance.

That October he got rave reviews for his work on the Heidelberg University sidelines from *The Advocate*:

"Caleb Sickles, the Indian who is remembered by every Newark baseball fan, as a star center fielder, is coaching the Heidelberg team and has developed the best team the Tiffin institution has ever had."

He later received accolades for keeping the Dennison game close when his players were outweighed by almost 40 pounds per man, and some of his best players were unable to play due to injuries sustained in the Ohio Medical College game.

Although he thought about heading west, Caleb set about rooting himself further in Seneca County, Ohio, for which Tiffin was the seat. A controversy rose in 1905 when he was elected delegate to the county convention, probably as a Republican. The issue was whether a non-citizen Indian who could not vote could hold an elected office. Indians as a group were not granted citizenship and the right to vote until 1924. Individual Indians had become citizens decades before that, when they received allotments in many cases.

Caleb's dental practice flourished, due in part, surely, to his fame as an athlete and coach. In the fall of 1905 he coached the Heidelberg team again and in November supported his alma mater when the Indians played the Massillon Tigers. In December, Caleb plunged into matrimony by marrying Mabel Teachnor, a white girl from Manchester he met in Columbus. She was about the same age as Caleb and had been a seamstress. The *Newark Daily Advocate* reported,

"'Sick' managed to keep the news of his wedding well concealed and escaped from Columbus before many of his numerous friends became aware of the fact that he had passed from the ranks of bachelordom. Dr. Sickles met his wife when attending O. M. U. She was connected then, it is said, with the Protestant Hospital."

Caleb established himself quite well in the dominant society of the community and freely shared his experiences with Carlisle students. The good people of Tiffin were also glad to have Caleb in their midst. The Heidelberg University school newspaper raved about his performance as their football coach:

"Heidel is proud of her teams and managers, but prouder of her loyal coach. Dr. Sickles needs no introduction to the athletic world, nor to the students of Heidelberg University. He is a perfect gentleman and a better football coach is nowhere to be found. He has the ability to work out new plays as well as to use old ones to a great advantage. He always has perfect control of his men, for they have confidence in him. The standard of athletics at Heidelberg has been raised fifty per cent since he has come to coach her teams. Three cheers for Coach Sickles!!"

In his history of the college, E. I. F. Williams gave Sickles credit for elevating Heidelberg's athletic program:

"The credit for this move should be given to Dr. C. M. Sickles, who had charge of coaching the athletic teams. No longer was the university janitor to be the football manager and students of penmanship the members of the teams. Heidelberg joined with other colleges in maintaining high standards of scholarship and sportsmanship in conducting the game as a prerequisite for a student['s] participation."

Caleb Sickles responded to Major Mercer's request for information from former athletes in 1907 and Moses Friedman's in 1909. His responses went into detail and he began a correspondence with the school that lasted until its closing. From this correspondence, we learn much about the man and his experiences. Dr. Sickles wrote a piece that was printed in the April 10, 1908, issue of *The Arrow* and is included in its entirety:

"Carlisle has done many things for me—good things. Entering when quite young my life was shaped there, it gave me an insight for higher things in life. When I left I strove four years to attain or rather fit myself for a useful life in the community in which I choose to live. I will advise every graduate of Carlisle to continue their studies. When you finish your course at Carlisle it is indeed a commencement—you are just beginning. Take up some special branch of work. A graduate of a technical school or of any special branch can always find employment and command a good salary. For my life work I chose a profession—that of dentistry. I put myself on a footing with the white man, struck out boldly in a small city of Ohio in competition with my white brothers, with nothing but my education and nerve. I am not eulogizing myself and do not want you to take it as such, I only want to set forth the facts that might help someone of my own race. I have so far succeeded in life although I have just begun. What I have done others of you can do. You may not all make a success in the 'tooth pulling' business but you can do something else equally as well. Since leaving school I have read considerably on the Indian question, which is no question at all. There may be no hope for the old Indians but the young men and women, there is plenty for them to do if they but would. The question is squarely up to you. The success you attain will depend upon yourself. Get away from the reservation and become a citizen of the United States. Work and your success is assured."

A month later an article titled, "Real Indian Joins Red Men" ran in *The Marion Daily Star*. Using more than a little irony, the reporter announced that Sickles, "... a former football star of national reputation, was among those initiated into the mysteries of the order [Improved Order of Red Men]." The very idea of an Indian joining a secret society of white men was newsworthy, let alone one that used Indian regalia in its ceremonies. Caleb was also a member of the Elks.

In 1909 he wrote again, this time about a different issue:

"I am doing all I can to live up to the standards taught me while at Carlisle. It is very hard for the Indian to succeed among the white people on account of race prejudice. I find it no handicap because very few know I have the strain of Indian blood in my veins, but I heard on all sides about this being a white man's country....God bless you and your co-workers in the good work they are doing."

The following year Caleb, at Friedman's invitation, had photos of his home and office taken to be published in Carlisle's literary journal, *The Red Man*. Included in the exterior photo were, from the right, his brother, Raymond, whom he was educating, Mabel and himself. Their

HOME OF C. M. SICKLES, CARLISLE '98
DR. SICKLES IS SUCCESSFULLY PRACTICING HIS PROFFESSION AT TIFFIN, OHIO

servant is probably included in the unnamed people in the photo. Sickles went into great detail about the demographics of the town, his practice and his financial situation, which was very good. He was contemplating building a new house in two years. He stated with pride that "... I have no little back room, one 'horse-shack,' that a decrier of Indian education would imagine." Recalling some personal history he stated, "I came here without a cent—besides being in debt several hundred dollars—now I have over 1,000.00 in cash in the banks here— This might seem as an object lesson to the other students there—that where there is a will, there is a way... P.S. The photographer's bill is 3.00."

Dr. Sickles at work

Caleb Sickles was doing very well indeed when one considers he was one of 15 dentists practicing in a town of 1,700 people. He wrote at length describing his practice:

> "At present I have all I can do which means I do a business of from 250.00 to 300.00 per mo. Gross. I started in, in debt and have gradually paid out—all the time adding to my office—now I have over 1,000.00 worth of furniture and instruments in my office—the accompanying photograph does not show all—as my laboratory does not show in the picture—among some of my instruments and machines— which are very expensive—I number—a Columbia electric engine with Dariot hand peice [sic]—(all cond) fountain cuspidor—Elgin casting machine, electric annealor—Columbia favorite chair—Sharp lamp—Electric lathe—gasoline blow pipe— just those articles represent an outlay of over 450.00. Then there are my countless smaller instruments aggregating over 500.00 more. My office is lighted by electricity."

Both dentists—Sickles and fellow Carlisle alum James Johnson—were doing very well and were proud of their accomplishments. Pratt surely considered them shining examples of what top students could achieve and very likely used them to promote Carlisle's value as an educational institution.

Caleb's next letter to Carlisle was one of sadness to Wallace and Nellie Denny. It was to inform them that Mabel had died. After telling the details of her last days he wrote, "I know she is in heaven for she was a pure woman." He wrote Superintendent Friedman a year later to offer his regrets for not being able to attend commencement and to philosophize.

> "It would be a grand thing if all the members of the Class of 1912 could attend college, which would give them a wider range of thought and fit them to fight the battles of the world....We all know there is room for the educated Indian—all we need is a chance. The proof is that today many Indians are holding responsible positions throughout our cities. Success to all of you."

Three years later he had better news. Caleb married Miss Nina M. Hankey on August 19, 1915, and visited Carlisle with his new bride on their honeymoon trip to Boston, New York, and other points in the East. Sickles was rightly proud of what he had accomplished including owning his own automobile and farm. His July 15, 1916 letter to Acting Superintendent John D. DeHuff discussed a possible visit to the Indian school and also announced the birth of their son, an 8¼-pound boy, on the 13th. The visit took place and Caleb likely gave the talk on proper dental care that was discussed in the letter.

America's entrance into WWI changed many people's plans, and so it was with Sickles. An almost-40-year old Caleb Sickles served as a 1st Lieutenant in the U. S. Army 11th Battalion and was discharged on December 24, 1918 at Fort Oglethorpe, Georgia. It is not clear whether Caleb enlisted or was drafted. Given his age, he probably volunteered. Regardless, he was inducted after the armistice was signed and served a very short time.

Caleb returned to his dental practice and did some coaching in the 1920s at the Tiffin Junior Home, an orphanage that was merged into the Tiffin State Hospital in 1944. The 1920 census listed Caleb as living on Webster Street with his wife, Nina M. (32), Caleb M. Jr. (3 years 5 months), and Ralph M. (1 year 9 months). They would have two more sons, Dewight and Eldon, as well as a daughter, Audrey.

A newspaper from the seat of nearby Allen County, *The Lima News,* recalled Caleb's exploits in a 1954 article:

> "The 1921 team defeated Chicago East Lane Tech, then recognized as national champion although averaging only 138-lbs per man. Passing was their game. In fact, Dee Gris threw one to John Starret for 80 yards and it still stands as a national record. Gris is now a Tiffin policeman and Starret, later to become coach, is now head of a large boys' club at Nashville, Tenn. Dr. Caleb Sickles, a local dentist and former player with the Carlisle Indians, coached such a complicated offense that the officials had to be briefed before each game and the Tiffin captain had to notify the referee before each play. As a pre-game feature, Starret and Gris would stand on the two 20-yard lines and heave passes back and forth, all of which had a rather demoralizing effect on the opposition."

Caleb must have maintained some ties with his family in Wisconsin as he owned land there until 1938. The local newspaper, the *Appleton Post-Crescent,* reported on Caleb Jr. selling a parcel in the town of Oneida that October. Now in his 60s, Caleb Sr. may have wanted to reduce his holdings to simplify his life. He died of a heart attack in Tiffin on January 30, 1950 at about 70 years of age.

Benjamin Skenandore

Ben Skenandore arrived at Carlisle on January 4, 1913 at age 20 and was placed in Room No. 9. He joined the YMCA and sang in a quartet at the March meeting. Already present on campus was Fred Skenandore, who was close in age to Ben. When only last names were given in school and newspaper articles, determining whether Ben or Fred was being referenced posed a challenge.

Ben went on his first outing in April. In late-July the team of horses pulling the mowing machine got away from Ben, catching him on the cutter bar. He convalesced for a week and paced himself after that. He returned to Carlisle at the end of August, in time for the start of the 1913-14 school year. A Skenandore played in a football game in

Name:	Benjamin Skenandore	Nickname: Ben
DOB:	6/23/1893	Height:
Weight:		Age: 20
Parents:	Joshua Skenandore Christine Skenandore	Home: West De Pere, WI
Early Schooling:	Oneida Boarding School Flandreau Indian School	
Later Schooling:	Ford Apprenticeship Program	

October, but which one? Fred was on outing and not on campus, so it couldn't have been him. It had to have been Ben. Either of them could have played in November, but only Ben could have done it in October.

Ben went on outing in late-May 1914 and again returned in time for the start of the new school year. Both Skenandores played in games for the Reserves that fall, Fred at halfback and Ben at tackle or end. Both went out for the track and lacrosse teams in spring 1915 and both played in the big April lacrosse win over Penn.

Both left for Detroit at the end of May to join the apprentice program at Ford Motor Company. They stayed in Detroit rather than returning to Carlisle in the fall. Both were promoted to the $5.00 a day level in December. Fellow Carlislian Joseph Gilman broke the factory record for assembling a Model T by five minutes. Some complained about too many football players getting Carlisle's coveted Ford apprenticeship slots but nothing seemed to change. When Henry Ford raised the salary he paid workers to $5.00 a day, it was twice what other employers were paying. This made working at Ford quite attractive to most working people.

While Ben was at Ford, his brother John initiated a series of letters in an attempt to sell him a red cow for $30. Superintendent Friedman punted the decision to J. C. Hart who was superintendent at Oneida. What finally happened wasn't recorded.

An article in *The Carlisle Arrow* titled "Ford 'Original Americans'" discussed the groups then working at Ford:

> "The two Oneidas from Wisconsin, Fred and Ben Skenandore, coming from a tribe which knows no annuities and whose members have had to work hard from childhood. Consequently Fred and Ben are among the hardest and best workers at the Ford factory. As of the year ending June 30, 1916, Fred had earned $805.20 and Ben $1,071.20. From those earnings they had saved $201.30 and $267.80, respectively."

Ben married Lucy Horne on July 17, 1916. Born in England, she was not an Oneida. His being married may have led to him being dropped from the Carlisle rolls on July 31, 1916. Even though he was married, he didn't stay with Ford. On March 2, 1917, G. W. Griswold of Ford Motor Company wrote Superintendent Lipps (Carlisle's administration had changed in 1914) complaining about Ben's resignation:

> "Skenandore claims that indoor work does not agree with him and that he has firmly made up his mind to return to his home in Wisconsin. We attempted to co-operate with him by suggesting a transfer to different work or otherwise adjust affairs here but he refused to allow us to do so."

Ben registered for the WWI draft on June 5, 1917. He listed his date of birth as June 23, 1893, one day earlier than what was given to Carlisle. He would have known what his own birthday was better than Indian Agency personnel did. He was living in Hobart, Wisconsin and working at the Interlake Pulp and Paper Company mill in Appleton, Wisconsin and was married.

Benjamin Skenandore died at his parents' home in Hobart on October 2, 1918 after battling tuberculosis for several years. He was survived by his wife, parents, and several siblings.

Fred Skenandore

Fred Skenandore arrived at Carlisle on November 5, 1908 at age 15 and was placed in first grade. His father had died some time before and his mother had married Jamison Metoxen. Already present at the school was Fred Schenandore, Onondaga from New York. Administrators confused the two Fred S's in publications and documents, sometimes spelling each of their last names the way the other's family name was spelled. Some documents in Oneida Fred's student file were actually Onondaga Fred's. The latter was best known for his track exploits and especially as a percussionist in the band. He left Carlisle for good in 1912 while Oneida Fred was still there. The school newspaper once referred to Oneida Fred as Fred Jr., probably because he was younger and had arrived more recently. This chapter focuses on him.

Name:	Fred Skenandore	Nickname:	Fredie
DOB:	1/18/1894	Height:	5'11"
Weight:	145 lbs.	Age:	18
Parents:	Sickles Skenandore Ida Skenandore	Home:	Oneida, WI
Early Schooling:	Oneida Boarding School		
Later Schooling:	Ford Apprenticeship Program US Army, mechanical drawing		

Fred spent the bulk of the 1908-09 school year on campus. He went on his first outing in summer 1909 near New Hope, Pennsylvania. His second outing, also in Bucks County, lasted almost all of the 1909-10 school year. After a summer in Carlisle, Fred spent the 1910-11 school year with the W. L. Lathrop family near New Hope. This outing generated his first two mentions in *The Carlisle Arrow* because he would be spending Christmas with the Lathrops. He spent the 1911 summer with Dr. G. M. Marshall in New Hope. In January 1912, he ran away for a week but returned to the Lathrops. The reason for him running away wasn't specified. He stayed there until mid-April. In June, he went out to J. H. Hoffman, RFD 8 Carlisle, where he stayed until football season. While on the varsity squad, he could only hope to get into games in which the starters had built up large enough leads that allowed scrubs to play. The Carlisle team was at its peak in the 1911-1912-1913 seasons, the best teams in Carlisle's history. He finished his five-year enrollment in mid-June 1913 and returned to Wisconsin.

His records to this time included no trade or industry, making it likely he was working on farms when on outings. The returned student form prepared in June for Friedman's signature but not signed included, "Weak Character but good disposition." This form recommended him for three possible positions: "1. Farmer, 2. General worker, 3. Wagon maker, 4. Left blank."

In August 1913, Assistant Disciplinarian Wallace Denny wrote Superintendent Friedman to recommending he not allow four students to be readmitted to the school. Fred Skenandore was one of the boys listed. Denny gave his reason for not wanting Fred back: "Fred Skenandore is also a thief. He is very white and has acted as a bootlegger among our boys." Friedman approved and signed a note at the bottom of the letter that said, "Referred to Mr. Meyer to see that recommendations are carried out." Next to Fred's name, someone—Meyer possibly—penciled in "Came back." When Denny wrote the letter he thought the four boys were at home. They must have returned and were readmitted before Meyer received Friedman's note.

With the trouble that led to his running away earlier apparently resolved, someone (Meyer?) allowed Fred to return. Fred was readmitted for a second five-year enrollment on November 8, 1913. Being on outing and not on campus, he couldn't have played in October games. It had to have been Ben Skenandore. Either of them could have played in November. Fred played on the lacrosse team in the spring and stayed on campus until June 29, 1914, when he went out to Robert Hoffman, RFD Carlisle again. He ran away for three weeks before returning this time. After that, he stayed on campus throughout the new school year. Both he and Ben played in games for the Reserves in 1914, he at halfback and Ben at tackle or end. Fred joined the carriage-making shop and became active in student organizations for the first time that year. Both went out for the track team in the spring. Both played in the lacrosse victory over Penn in April..

Both left for Detroit at the end of May to join the apprentice program at Ford Motor Company. They stayed in Detroit rather than returning to Carlisle in the fall. Both were promoted to the $5.00 a day level in December. Fellow Carlislian Joseph Gilman broke the factory record for assembling a Model T by five minutes. Some complained about so many of Carlisle's coveted Ford apprenticeship slots were given to football players. When Henry Ford raised the salary he paid workers to $5.00 a day, it was twice what other employers were paying. This made working at Ford quite attractive to most working people.

An article in *The Carlisle Arrow* titled "Ford 'Original Americans'" discussed the groups then working at Ford:

> "The two Oneidas from Wisconsin, Fred and Ben Skenandore, coming from a tribe which knows no annuities and whose members have had to work hard from childhood. Consequently Fred and Ben are among the hardest and best workers at the Ford factory."

As of the year ending June 30, 1916, Fred had earned $805.20 and Ben $1,071.20. From those earnings they had saved $201.30 and $267.80, respectively. Having finished his course some months earlier, Fred was transferred to Ford's Kansas City branch in February 1917, bringing an end to his time at Carlisle. He related his situation to his former schoolmates, "...owing to the lack of stock from the factory at

Detroit, the work is not so heavy and there are more frequent layoffs....Therefore I am not making as much as I was in Detroit."

With the US entering WWI that spring, Fred registered for the draft on June 5, 1917. On his registration card, he claimed his mother, two sisters, and a brother as being dependent on him. He curiously listed himself as a native in box 4 and Caucasian in box 10. Like some other Carlisle students, he listed his time at the school as being in military service. He must have signed up, or was drafted, not too long after that because his name appeared in Carlisle's Roll of Honor, a long list of former Carlisle students then serving in the Army, Navy, or Marines the school published in the December 21, 1917 edition of *The Carlisle Arrow and Red Man*.

On March 5, 1918, Fred boarded a special train as part of the Kansas City portion of the last western Missouri contingent of the first draft of WWI. Local draft board officials said Skenandore was the finest physical specimen they had examined.

On March 20, 1918 Fred wrote Wallace and Nelly Denny, administrators at Carlisle, that he was attending Medical Officers Training Camp (MOTC) at Fort Riley, Kansas. "I have been here now for two weeks and surely like it. I was in the competitive drilling team and took second place. I am taking a special course in mechanical drawing on all motors and gas engines. I have taken out a $10,000 insurance policy which I am proud of."

In July, Corporal Skenandore, who was assigned to Field Hospital 40, was on the passenger list for the SS *Darro* out of New York. Precisely what he did at the field hospital isn't known but the facts he had gone through the Ford apprenticeship program and he had taken a course on automobile engines suggest he was a mechanic who maintained ambulances and other vehicles. He returned as Private Skenandore on the *Kaiserin Auguste Victoria*, a German ocean liner that was ceded to Great Britain as war reparations, to Hoboken, New Jersey from Brest, France on June 10, 1919. Whether he was busted from corporal to private or the corporal was a typographical error is unknown.

On September 8, Fred and Willa J. Lemmon, both 23, married in Kansas City, Missouri. They likely knew each other before the war. He continued to work for Ford there. By 1930, the Skenandores had relocated to Dearborn, Michigan to work at the Ford plant. In the 1940s, he had shifted to Packard and was living at 432 Horton Street in Detroit. In 1950, he was working as a general clerk for a retail warehouse and they were living in Detroit. Fred Skenandore died in 1973 at the VA Hospital in Wood, Wisconsin at 79 years of age. Willa survived him but they had no children. His grave marker listed him as "Wisconsin, Pvt US Army, World War I."

Thomas Skenandore

Thomas Amos Skenandore arrived at Carlisle on March 23, 1888 at 12 years of age to start a five-year enrollment. He spent his summers at farms on outings. No mention was recorded of his academic standing or trade. After completing his enrollment on June 30, 1993, he went home. He returned on October 8 to start a second term of indefinite duration.

Something else happened in October 1893: Superintendent Pratt rescinded his ban on football games against other schools, resulting in a hastily prepared schedule of three games. It isn't clear if Thomas was on the team or not. The next year, he wasn't a regular but, in1895 he was a starter at guard or tackle.

His father requested he be released, probably because he was needed at home. He was discharged for good on May 18, 1896. The next

Name:	Thomas A. Skenandore	Nickname:	Tom
DOB:	9/25/1874	Height:	5'10½"
Weight:	172 lbs.	Age:	18
Parents:	Jacob Skenandore Mary Skenandore	Home:	De Pere, WI
Early Schooling:	Oneida Boarding School		
Later Schooling:			

year, Thomas married Zippa Metoxen, a Carlisle alum who had taken nurses training in Connecticut after graduating from Carlisle in 1894.

In addition to doing farm work, he made a little, very little, playing football. Unknown is when he started and stopped. However, it is documented that he played halfback for the Green Bay team. He was the only paid player on the undefeated 1897 team that claimed the world championship. The defeat of Lawrence College highlighted the season. They also beat Marinette, Oconto, Fond du Lac, and other towns in the area by using the infamous Flying Wedge.

GREEN BAY GRIDDERS OF LATE NINETIES

Top row, left to right—Burns, Krippner, Vandenberg; second row, Hulbert, Van den Brook, Groesbeck, Johnson; third—F. Flatley, Gray, Silverwood, Skenandore, J. Flatley; bottom row, Pies, Gross (mascot) Hanrahan.

In 1900 Thomas and Zippa lived and worked on a farm they didn't own and had one son, Hilton. By 1910 they had moved onto land of their own on Duck Creek Road with their three sons and four daughters. They owned 45 acres of which 12 acres were cleared for farming. They lived in an eight-room house Thomas built. In addition to housekeeping, Zipp raised poultry.

Zippa Metoxen Skenandore sent this postcard photo of her four daughters to Nellie Denny at Carlisle Indian School in 1912 (or 1910. The last digit isn't distinct.).

They sent the older two children to Tomah Indian School, a government boarding school in Wisconsin. In 1912, they enrolled oldest child, Hilton, at Carlisle. Thomas took a lumbering job at Lac du Flambeau, Wisconsin. That work was expected to last until 1914. Hilton's sister Elizabeth joined him at Carlisle in 1915 and Madeline in 1917. Both were sent home rather than to another government school when Carlisle was closed in August 1918.

In 1917, Zippa requested Hilton's early return to help on the farm as his father was too sick to do the work. She had to wait until Hilton completed his term and travel funds became available in July.

In 1920 their farm was mortgaged and five of their children lived with them. Thomas sold a 16-acre parcel to Mike Coffey, possibly to pay off debts. In November 1921 his 17.5-acre lot in Oneida was put up for sheriff's sale for unpaid taxes. In 1922, the day after his daughter Madeline married John E. Moore, Thomas transferred the farm to Madeline and her husband and moved to Milwaukee.

Thomas died for unspecified reasons on April 14, 1925. Zippa lived until 1933.

Lewis Webster

Lewis Webster arrived at Carlisle on August 28, 1891 at 12 years of age to start a five-year enrollment. His physical description mentioned a noticeable scar on his head. Some documents spelled his name as Louis. Prior schooling wasn't mentioned but it was common for Oneida children to attend the Oneida Boarding School before progressing to other schools. His student file contained nothing about the academic or trades work he did at the school. He went on outings to farms for the summers of 1896 through 1899. He was discharged in June 1900 with no mention as to why he stayed so long without reenrolling.

He got little mention, a lot less than his siblings received, in school publications but he did get one. Lewis must have joined the Invincible Debating Society because, the April 10, 1896 edition of *The Indian Helper* included the paragraph:

Name:	Lewis Earl Webster	Nickname:	Lewis Sr., Louis
DOB:	3/25/1879	Height:	4'8"
Weight:		Age:	12
Parents:	Simon Webster Electra Webster	Home:	De Pere, WI
Early Schooling:	Oneida Boarding School?		
Later Schooling:			

"Bruce Patterson and Lewis Webster enacted a scene from 'The Lost Pig' as part of the program in the monthly meeting held in the YMCA building. Lewis drew on the blackboard, a stately and well rounded animal of the swine species. Talking as he chalked."

In September 1897 he began working in the print shop.

Players on the Second Team, Third Team, Reserves, and Scrubs seldom received any press coverage. However, he was mentioned as having played in one particular game. In 1898 Lewis played left tackle on the Second Team which drubbed the Carlisle All-Collegiates 40-0. This was Pop Warner's first year at Carlisle and they had their best team to date. The competition for playing time had to have been fierce. Making the Second Team would have been an achievement. He was probably on the squad previous to 1898 but no documentation has been found to support that.

In 1900 *The Bucks County Gazette* noticed his departure from Carlisle: "Genus Baird and Lewis Webster, two young Oneida Indians, well known in this vicinity [for having worked on outings in Bucks County], have recently returned to their homes in Wisconsin." That year Lewis's name appeared in two places on the US Census: Carlisle Indian School and Bucks County, both in Pennsylvania.

Lewis began working on a farm, for Albert Prouty most likely, almost immediately after he returned to Wisconsin in 1900. He married an Oneida woman, Marie Christjohn, in October 1906. Her proper name was Mary but she went by Marie.

In 1907, he reputedly played end for the Frankford Athletic Club, one of the better semi-pro teams of that time, from Franklin, Pennsylvania. Franklin defeated the Carlisle Reserves 10–0 in a mud game in November. Coming east to play football during harvest time would have been difficult for a married man. The pay wasn't likely great. If it was, the possibility of Lewis doing it increased. He probably wasn't being confused with the other Lewis/Louis Webster, the Omaha who was then at Carlisle. That Lewis Webster was just 17 and wouldn't likely have been physically mature enough to play on a semi-pro team. Also, Carlisle newspapers covered the game, which would have made Indian School officials aware of Webster having played professionally, something they would have frowned upon. Another explanation is that someone else, possibly a college boy, was playing under Webster's name. Carlisle had such a cachet at the time, using it may have increased the pay an imposter got for the game.

June 23, 1910 Lewis Webster, who had been employed by Albert Prouty as a hired man on his farm had shifted to working at O. Goodell in Hill Point. This was probably a sawmill because he claimed to having worked at them since returning from Carlisle.

Webster entered Indian Service in 1911 at Lac du Flambeau Boarding School where he was the Disciplinarian. He claimed to own land worth $2,000 at Oneida. In 1913 he invited Carlisle Superintendent Friedman to go fishing with him. In 1915 he wrote the superintendent that he enjoyed his work and then had a five-year-old son, Lewis Jr.

In 1920, Lewis and Marie were still at Lac du Flambeau. He was a government agency farmer and she was a laundress. They had a son and two daughters at this time. In 1921 Lewis made a land swap of some sort with Martin McCormick.

By 1923 They were at Haskell Institute in Lawrence, Kansas. For how long isn't know but they could have been there five years at the most. In 1926 they were both working at the Indian School in Mt. Pleasant, Michigan where Lewis was a boys advisor and Marie was a matron. They were there at least through 1930 and probably until they retired from the Indian Service.

By 1940, they were living with oldest son, Lewis Jr. in rural Green Bay along with their two youngest children, Kenneth and Dorothy. Lewis Jr. was single and was employed as a stevedore for a transfer company. Business must have been slow because he was seeking work at the time. Lewis Sr. gardened his own land and Marie worked as a laundress at a hospital.

When he registered for the WWII draft in 1942 at age 63, Lewis Sr. was working for Cargill Elevator in Green Bay while living in Oneida. In 1950, Lewis was retired from farming but they were caring for a foster child.

Marie died in 1951. Lewis remarried to the former Electra Cornelius in 1958. He died on June 23, 1964 at 85 years of age.

23

Hugh & Joel Wheelock

If the Carlisle Indian School had a first family, it would have been the Wheelocks. Brothers Dennison and James Riley Wheelock were students who, at different times, later held the bandmaster position and made the Carlisle Indian School Band famous. Among other things, Dennison composed two marches named after the Carlisle school. Both Dennison and James attended Dickinson College Preparatory School after completing their Carlisle studies. After leaving government service, they formed Indian bands of their own and traveled around the country. After contracting tuberculosis, Dennison set aside his baton and took up the law, spending much time in Washington, DC. Laurence M. Hauptman related that many Oneidas today regard Dennison as "apple," red on the outside and white on the inside for his land dealings.

Sister Ida was quite active in school organizations such as the Susan Longstreth Literary Society. Several other Wheelocks were mentioned prominently in Carlisle publications but were probably cousins. Football star Martin Wheelock comes quickly to mind. But there were also Wheelocks who played football as well as making music with the band and on Carlisle's vaunted varsity. For example, musician James Wheelock led a shop team, but that team didn't play against other schools. However, his younger brothers did.

Name:	Joel Howard Wheelock	Nickname:	
DOB:	10/7/1890	Height:	5'9"
Weight:	160 lbs.	Age:	22
Parents:	James A. Wheelock Sophia Wheelock (stepmother)	Home:	West De Pere, WI
Early Schooling:	unknown		
Later Schooling:	Lebanon Valley College Preparatory School		

Joel Howard and Hugh Coleman Wheelock were younger brothers of Dennison, James and Ida, children of James A. Wheelock. Their lives were so intertwined that including both in a single chapter makes things clearer. Why their self-reported birthdates are less than nine months apart is anyone's guess. The May 1, 1896 edition of *The Indian Helper* reported that Sophia Metoxen Wheelock had died recently, leaving James Sr. with several small children to raise. Wheelock Sr. was known to Superintendent Pratt because he had visited Dennison, James and Ida during commencement.

Sophia, however, probably wasn't their mother, because she was only eight years older than Dennison. Also, there was a seven-year gap between daughters Ida and Louisa. The older children, Dennison through Ida, must have been from the first wife. James Sr. must have remarried and had the younger ones with Sophia. Hugh's enrollment papers list James A. Wheelock as his father and Sophia as his mother. However, Joel's papers list his father as deceased due to old age and his mother as having died in childbirth. These differences may may been due in part to the month difference between the boys' enrollments. Their father remarried after the death of Sophia to his third wife, the former Lena Webster, and had children with her, too. 1905 censuses suggested that he died around that time leaving his older minor children as orphans. His younger minor children remained with their mother, who soon married Martin Wheelock. This lack of a name change for her confuses those who try to decipher the Wheelock family tree. The boys' guardian was their older half-brother, Dennison. At the time they came to Carlisle, each had four living brothers and five living sisters in good health. One brother had died of alcoholism and a sister had died of tuberculosis. Hugh, sometimes called Hughie J. on the census, and Joel enrolled at Carlisle in 1905 on September 7 and October 8, respectively and, at times, had an older sibling on campus, sometimes as bandmaster.

Like most children attending Carlisle, their names did not start showing up in school publications immediately upon arrival. Joel's name first appeared in the fall of 1908; Hugh's came later. Most of Joel's early mentions were for athletics, such as leading the "Devils" to victory in a football game played between his shop, the Printers, and the Blacksmiths. The following January, he played on the school's first inter-scholastic basketball team. In the spring, he earned his letter "C" in track by placing 4th in the 120-yard hurdles at the state intercollegiate track meet held in Harrisburg. He even raked in prizes at the 4th of July track meet held at the school as part of the festivities. Joel won a pair of running shoes for winning the 120-yard high hurdles for boys over 15 years old. He also won two dozen oranges for winning the 220-yard dash and another dozen for his share of the prize for placing 2nd in the 100-yard three-legged race with partner Joseph Loudbear. Lastly, he won a pair of tennis shoes for winning the 220-yard wheelbarrow race with teammates John Goslin and Levi Williams. Joel made quite a haul.

In late September 1909, Hugh Wheelock returned from outing and rejoined the football squad late. Joel had already run for a long touchdown a week before in the Hotshots' (that year's name for the Second Team) game against Steelton. That fall Joel got considerable playing time as a halfback, generally at right halfback, and "showed up well" until he twisted his knee in the Bucknell game. He recovered and got into the game with Syracuse, then made the trip to St. Louis to play in that game. A post-season description said that, at 18, he was the youngest man on the team.

Name:	Hugh Coleman Wheelock	Nickname:	Huge, Chief
DOB:	3/2/1891	Height:	5'10"
Weight:	172 lbs.	Age:	22
Parents:	James A. Wheelock Sophia Wheelock (stepmother)	Home:	West De Pere, WI
Early Schooling:	unknown		
Later Schooling:			

Joel Wheelock, 1912   Hugh Wheelock, 1910

Joel wrote a piece entitled "My Trip to Washington" for *The Carlisle Arrow* about traveling to the nation's capitol to play George Washington University. He also was credited as being part of the force that printed *The Arrow* and *The Indian Craftsman* and later for doing part of the composition on the program for the Athletic Banquet program. He played a clarinet solo for his class meeting and was elected captain of the Sophomores' basketball team. He was an all-around man about campus.

To further that image in early January 1910, Joel won first prize in the two-step dance contest with Sara Hoxie as his partner at the Carlisle Indian Band reception. In the spring, he continued to compete in several track events, gaining an occasional 1st place, and earning his second letter on the cinder path. At commencement, he was awarded his industrial certificate as a compositor, but he remained in school. If anything, he expanded his range of extra-curricular activities to include the Invincible Debating Society without dropping any existing activities. He was made an officer both for his Junior Class (after commencement) and by the Invincibles. He even recited "The American Flag" at a Saturday evening school social.

The following autumn the Wheelock boys were back out on the gridiron; Hugh didn't yet get significant playing time, but Joel did—enough to earn his first letter in football. *The Philadelphia Public Ledger* was quite impressed with his play: "In [Pete] Hauser and [Joel] Wheelock they found backs of the heavy, slashing, plunging type that are as good as any playing in the East today." Although Carlisle failed to win any of its big games in 1910, Joel received frequent kudos for his play. One that stands out was from the *Philadelphia Press*:

> "Wheelock was another Indian who played a spectacular game. He was able to gain through the line many times, and was strong on defensive play. Wheelock shone particularly at recovering Hauser's long forward passes, standing directly beyond center with his back toward the opponent's goal and by superhuman strength, keeping off Penn men until he had the ball safe in his arms."

In 1911, Joel took time out from his responsibilities as captain of the track team to play in the band, to give clarinet solos to class meetings, to serve as an officer of the Invincibles and of his class, to serve as Lt. Governor of the Model Government afternoon session, and, in the spring, to give his first speech as a Senior, "The Price of Success."

In February, for an assembly of the entire school, Hugh Wheelock performed in "*Brahmin, Jackal and Tiger*, a three-act comedy with a good moral, artistic, and up to the jungle standard of acting." After spending his summer at home, Hugh returned to school in September, when *The Arrow* reported, "The Seniors are rejoicing over the return of Joel Wheelock, who spent a most profitable vacation in Canada." It failed to mention exactly what he did during that vacation.

Both boys excelled in extra-curricular activities, but neither impressed his vocational instructor. E. K. Miller rated Joel's ability as a compositor as "Fair–Slow" although he considered him a willing worker with excellent behavior. Hugh's instructor was less kind, rating his ability as "not much good as a carpenter."

Hugh and Joel both made the varsity for 1911, arguably Carlisle's strongest team. However, with the return of Jim Thorpe and the maturation of some younger players, neither became a regular starter. However, injuries to regulars gave both of them opportunities, and they made the most of them. Joel stood out as right halfback—wingback in Warner's scheme—against Georgetown: "Wheelock was especially strong in helping to block opponents upon plays around his end of the line." Both got into the games and played well against the two Big Four teams the Indians defeated that year, Penn and Harvard. *The Carlisle Arrow* bragged,

"The Carlisle line out-charged and out-played Harvard in every spot, and it was the Indian forwards who made it possible for the backs to gain. Carlisle was without the service of Captain Burd [sic], our star end, and Newashe was in such condition that he only played a short time, but the Wheelock brothers, Joel and 'Huge,' filled their positions so well that there was no apparent weakness anywhere in the line."

Hugh played left tackle in both games, but Joel was needed at right end to stop the Crimson. *The Pittsburg Dispatch* summed up the season in its coverage of the Pitt game: "However, Thorpe wasn't the entire works; there were a few others, white men as well as Indians. Newashe and Arcasa were some stars themselves, so were Powell and Wheelock." Both Wheelock brothers got into enough games and played well enough to letter that year.

Hugh must have joined the Standard Debating Society at some time because he and Cora Bresette won a prize, most likely for dancing, at the New Year's Mercer-Standard reception. "Huge" was also active with the YMCA, giving a talk at the April volunteer meeting. Hugh, along with several others, spent the summer of 1912 working at a large brickworks in Mt. Union, Pennsylvania and improving the quality of the town band. Known today for being the home of the biggest Easter grass factory in the U. S., at that time, Mt. Union, located 45 miles southeast of Altoona, claimed to be the world's largest manufactory of silica bricks. Hugh didn't return to his studies that fall. Instead, he eloped to Cumberland, Maryland to marry a Mt. Union girl, Hattie E. Crubb, and continued to work at the brickworks and play in the town band. That fall he coached the town's newly formed high school football team. *The Arrow* did not give any information about his bride. It did report on his visit to the school and attendance at the game at Franklin Field in Philadelphia. They divorced in 1916 for desertion.

Joel was even more heavily involved in extra-curricular activities in 1912 than he had been in previous years. He started the new year as the "star" of the Easterners vs. Westerners football game and was elected captain for 1912. A week or so later, he sang "Silent Night" in a quartet accompanied by a lantern light show for a YMCA-YWCA Union meeting. A week after that, he and Joseph Saracino debated successfully the proposition, "That Richard III was a worse monarch than Charles II," at a meeting of the Invincibles. The following week, also with the Invincibles, he delivered the declamation, "The Boss Sees You." And, of course, he competed in track again.

At commencement, Joel Wheelock's name was listed alongside those of other star athletes in the class of 1912, his class, that included future College Football Hall-of-Famers Gus Welch and Jim Thorpe. The Commencement Issue of *The Arrow* included a short poem he wrote:

Music is the art of prophets

When J. W. hath forgot his notes,
he makes as though a crumb were in
his throat.

Joel again played football in the fall of 1912 but didn't get as much playing time as before on what was another powerhouse Carlisle team. *The Arrow* summarized his season: "Joel Wheelock is 5 ft. 9 in. tall, weighs 160 pounds, and is 22 years old. He is an Oneida from Wisconsin. Joel won his "C" by his work in the backfield when he relieved some regulars in important games. All he lacked to make a first-class back was fighting spirit and he showed considerable of this in the latter part of the—season."

Even though he had graduated and was now taking a commercial course, Joel continued his usual dizzying array of extra-curricular activities throughout the school year and gained an additional responsibility when he was promoted to captain of a set of troops. *The Arrow* commented a couple of times on his leadership. First: "It seems that everybody takes notice of Captain Wheelock's troop as they march over to the Dining Room." Then later: "If they keep up their good work, Captain Wheelock and his troop will receive some notice at the inaugural parade."

After completing the commercial course at Carlisle, Joel enrolled at the preparatory school for Lebanon Valley College (LVC) in Annville, Pennsylvania where he—big surprise—also played football and ran track for the Dutchmen. Down 10-0 against the Carlisle Reserves, he donned a uniform, and according to the *1915 Bizarre*, "His presence fired the entire team with enthusiasm and for the first time during the game they showed what they were capable of doing." He quickly scored two touchdowns to snatch a victory from the Indian Second Team. Shortly after that the *Manitoba Free Press* (Canadian papers often ran article about Carlisle sports) ran a short critique: "Joe [sic] Wheelock, the famous Carlisle star of other years, is playing end [sic] for Lebanon Valley. Evidently Lebanon Valley plays them to a ripe old age." In a losing effort against Bucknell, he made a gutsy performance. LVC's newspaper, *College News*, reported, "Wheelock, although playing with a twisted ankle, a knee in not any too good shape, and a nose very nearly broken, stuck to his place and played his hardest during the whole time." He not only ran the ball for touchdowns and up the middle for tough yardage, but he was also their kicker. When in Lebanon, Joel probably played in Tyrrell's Military Band when his schedule allowed. He had friends from Carlisle who did, and he surely was acquainted with George F. Tyrrell.

Joel Wheelock in track uniform

In the winter and spring, he played basketball and ran track in their respective seasons. Joel visited Carlisle several times during the school year. Could he have left a girlfriend behind? In August, he wrote Superintendent Lipps asking for trainfare from Mt. Union, where he had been working that summer, to Carlisle to assist Pop Warner with the football team. Lipps did not receive the request well: "Athletics are being conducted differently at Carlisle than has been the custom and no inducements whatever can be held out to students who desire to be enrolled or to former students who desire to return to school for the purpose outlined in your letter." He would not be coaching at Carlisle so he returned to Annville to play for LVC.

In October 1914, Lebanon Valley College beat Gettysburg for the first time in 20 years due, in great part, to halfback Wheelock's efforts both in smashing through the line and skirting its ends. Joel was named to the All-Pennsylvania backfield at the end of the season. In December, *College News* included Henry L. Wilder's selections for the "All-Time-All-Lebanon Valley team." After just two seasons with the Dutchmen, Joel was named left halfback on the first team of LVC's all-time greats. A couple of months later, he was appointed assistant coach for the Blue and White for the upcoming year.

Joel's weekends were filled with football in 1915, assisting with the coaching for Lebanon Valley College on Saturdays and playing for the Altoona Indians semi-pro team on Sundays. He was joined in Altoona by his brother, Hugh. Due to the close proximity between Mt. Union and Altoona, it may have been Hugh who arranged for the two to play alongside several of their old Carlisle teammates. The Wheelock brothers played for Altoona again in 1916.

By June 1917, when they registered for the WWI draft, both Joel and Hugh had found gainful employment, if only for the summer. Joel worked as a tool and die maker at the Bethlehem Steel plant in Lebanon, Pennsylvania and Hugh was working for Harbison Walker Brick Co. and was a deputy sheriff in Mt. Union but was then single. His 1912 marriage had ended in divorce for desertion in 1916.

According to his obituary, Joel served in the Navy as a pharmacist's mate during WWI but, before joining up, served as the head football coach at LVC for the 1917 season. This was quite a feat for a student still in the prep school. According to the *The Quittapahilla 1919*:

> "The success of the season depended on 'Chief' and he did his best which was excellent. He was unbiased in picking men for their respective positions. He gave them new plays which were very effective, also new tactics on the defence that helped a great deal. 'Chief' had the faculty of bawling you out when you didn't do the right thing, but that only made you fight the harder. On the whole he was a good coach and deserves praise for developing such a fine squad out of so many raw recruits, for we must remember that only a few of our last year's Varsity men came back this year."

The school's yearbook recorded 1917 as a 3-4 season but cfbdatawarehouse.com included two more games, a forfeit by Temple and a 73–0 thrashing of Millersburg, giving Wheelock a 5–4 record for his only year as a head coach.

It is not known what Hugh did during that time period, although he did likely serve in the military because he was later a member of the VFW. After the war, Joel organized an All-Indian band which toured widely. Musicians in his large band included former Carlisle students, one of whom was James Garvie. His grandson, Jay Garvie, has a large photograph in which his grandfather is sitting in the front row. Wheelock is dressed in Oneida regalia including a war bonnet. A photo album donated to the Cumberland County Historical Society by William Winneshiek's granddaughter included several individual photographs taken of Wheelock's band members while the band was in Cincinnati in 1929. The musicians were wearing their tribal regalia just as they did when performing.

The 1920 census listed Hugh as divorced, living in Lewistown, Pennsylvania and working as a helper in an ice plant. Hugh married a widow, Mary Ann "Annie" Halbert, in Harrisburg in 1925. This was a second marriage for both of them. In 1930, Hugh, 36, was living in Lewistown but was then working as a laborer at the steel works.

Joel died at the Navy Hospital in Brooklyn, New York after a year and a half illness on February 17, 1932. Impressive military rites were performed by Oneida Indian World War I veterans at his funeral in

Oneida, Wisconsin. His wife, two brothers, and two sisters survived him..

"Chief" Wheelock, Hugh, was well-known in western Pennsylvania for playing bass and tenor drums in various bands including the Tyrone Division (of the Pennsylvania Railroad) band and his brother Joel's All-Indian band, the Veterans Of Foreign Wars Band, and the Methodist Church orchestra. He traveled with the J. E. Eshchew Rodeo Indian Band during the 1939–40 season. He worked as a bricklayer's helper at Standard Steel Works in Burnham for his day job. In April 1941, he joined the Marines as a snare drummer.

Hugh Wheelock died in November 1943, in Lewistown, Pennsylvania, a week after having a gangrenous appendix removed. He was recovering well and was expected to be discharged from the hospital when he was stricken fatally. His cause of death was listed as coronary occlusion.

The Wheelocks were the family who arguably best represented the things that made the Carlisle Indian School famous: its band and its football team. Other band members, such as James Garvie and William Winneshiek, played football on shop or band teams, or in Winneshiek's case, the NFL, but didn't make the varsity starting line-up. The Wheelocks were unique in that regard.

Martin Wheelock

Martin Frederick Wheelock was probably a cousin of the Wheelock musicians, who figured so prominently in Carlisle Indian School life. Martin's father was a Civil War veteran having served in the 3rd Wisconsin Volunteers. His mother died when he was about five years old. Martin arrived at Carlisle with a group of Oneidas led by Peter Powlas on September 20, 1890, when he was about 16 years old. Three years later, when Superintendent Pratt relented and allowed the boys to play football against other schools, Martin Wheelock was ready to compete.

By 1896, the team and its players were getting positive press. In *Harper's Weekly,* Caspar Whitney raved, "There is not a stronger nor heavier line in the country than that of the Indians, the centre and guards, Wheelock and B. Pierce, particularly being well-nigh impregnable." By September 1897, the school newspaper considered him one of the team's "big guns" and expressed concern that his ankle sprain might

Name:	Martin Frederick Wheelock	Nickname:	
DOB:	6/5/1874	Height:	6'1½"
Weight:	220 lbs.	Age:	27
Parents:	Abram Wheelock Mary Hill Wheelock	Home:	Green Bay, WI
Early Schooling:	unknown		
Later Schooling:	Haskell Institute		

be serious. Apparently it wasn't because in October he received a hero's welcome for playing well in a losing effort against a powerful opponent:

> "On Monday morning after breakfast, the football team, who returned the evening before from the Yale game which was played at New York last Saturday, was treated to a free ride across the parade, in the large four horse herdic, drawn by the entire battalion. Capt. Pierce, Frank Cayou, Frank Hudson, and Martin Wheelock occupied the small phaeton drawn by boys, and went in advance of the others. The band played lively marches, as handkerchiefs waved and mouths shouted. The demonstration was a great surprise to all making a unique scene for such an early morning hour. The school is proud of the record made for clean playing, and were gratified that the boys scored."

In November, Martin was injured in a game played in New York City against Brown University. Apparently the idea of taking a then new technology to diagnose an Indian was newsworthy as a press account of the incident was circulated nationally:

USES "X RAY" ON AN INDIAN.

Right Tackle of Carlisle Football Eleven Examined for Injuries.

> "Martin Wheelock, right tackle of the Carlisle, football eleven, a big Indian, six feet high, became acquainted with the latest acquisition to the white man's science, the X-ray, in the J. Hood Wright Memorial Hospital at New York City.
>
> "During the game with Brown, Wheelock had plunged headlong into a mass play directed against him. He tried to rise, but his right shoulder prevented. It was decided to try the X-ray on Wheelock, to see the exact injury done to his shoulder.
>
> "Wheelock was deeply interested in the performance. The bones in his hand were shown him, and he was delighted. Then

the ray was turned on his injured shoulder, and it was plainly seen he had suffered a fracture. The physicians declared that the man was the finest specimen of humanity they had ever seen.

"The hospital authorities believe that Wheelock will be able to play again during the present season."

With only two weeks left in Carlisle's season, the report was overly optimistic that he would be back in action that year. But he was able to continue his studies and complete the school year.

After vacationing at home in Wisconsin that summer, Martin returned, undaunted, to play again in 1898 and again helped to establish Carlisle's reputation. At season's end when Frank Hudson declined re-election as captain, Wheelock accepted the honor. Earlier that month he had been elected President of the Invincible Debating Society, an organization in which he participated actively the rest of his time at Carlisle. He "maintained the dignity befitting his office, and rendered wise decisions."

Martin Wheelock reclining on right

In May, Martin accepted another challenge as reported by *The Indian Helper*:

"Captain Martin Wheelock of the football team has been detailed as captain for the small boys' company, and assistant to Mrs. Given. While the football management may try his metal, his position as captain of the small boys will try his manhood, and for that reason is a position to be sought for and to hold if possible. The Man-on-the-band-stand wishes him success."

1899 was Pop Warner's first year at Carlisle. Perhaps it was his idea or maybe it was Captain Wheelock's to hold light practices in cool August evenings to prepare football candidates who happened to be on campus for the season. Whether it was Warner's coaching, the Carlisle players' maturing or, more likely, both, the Indians posted their best season to date. Martin's leadership surely contributed to the team's success. The team's two losses were to Harvard and Princeton. Some thought Carlisle would have defeated Harvard, had Martin been able to play. He was injured in the first half and carried off the field on a stretcher. Examined at the hospital, he was not seriously enough injured to be admitted. Walter Camp placed him on his All America Second Team for his efforts throughout the season.

In March, Martin Wheelock took on another adult task when he was a pallbearer for Miss Bessie Barclay, a teacher who succumbed to "rheumatic and stomach trouble." He reprised that role in an even sadder situation in May at the funeral for Paul, the ten-month-old son of band director Dennison Wheelock and his wife, Louise. Perhaps needing a break from sadness, he took a short vacation at a resort in the mountains near Pen Mar, Maryland, after which he returned to school ready for action.

Ed Rogers captained the 1900 team, and Martin Wheelock was still fighting in the trenches. He also did most of the punting, kicking off, and goal kicking that year. Initially Hawley Pierce was to captain the 1901 team but complaints regarding eligibility were raised. *The Fort Wayne News* complained, "Hawley Pierce, captain of the Carlisle Indian team, has held that office for several years, there being no limit as to the time a man may play on the team of reformed scalpers." It's not clear if such criticisms, offers to play professionally, or injury were the source of complaints against Pierce, but Martin Wheelock was selected to captain the Indians again.

That season had to have been difficult for Wheelock because he and Jimmie Johnson were the only regular starters who returned from the previous year. Big things were expected from Nelson Hare and

Charles Dillon because they had some experience. This was Carlisle's last losing season until the decline that began after the 1914 congressional inquiry. But Martin Wheelock still played his hardest and was again rewarded by Walter Camp. As in 1899, he was placed on Camp's All America Second Team.

At his commencement in February for the Class of 1902, Martin was asked to give one of the addresses. The subject of the talk was "The Indian as an Athlete." In his talk, Wheelock said:

> "The records of colonial times show that he [the Indian] is a born athlete. His very mode of living as a hunter and a warrior, develop his reasoning power, enabling him to plan his campaigns skillfully. The only thing that he lacked for many years has been a knowledge of the real cause of his loss of strength.
>
> "The Indian youth does not differ much from his white brother in his way of displaying energy and spirit. He had games of his own in which he took as much interest as the pale faces do in their modern sports. Since he has been taken away from his favorite hunting grounds and placed in the remote corners of the country called reservations, he seems to have lost his vigorous manhood. Why is this? Because he has been thrust back into the infant's cradle and bound with limits as a child is bound with clothes when put to sleep. It has caused him to neglect his physical development until he has lost nearly all the energy he displayed before the right of self-guidance was taken from him...
>
> "Since being placed in schools he has been obliged to come into close contact with many classes of people. In recent years, the Indian has been competing with his new friends in sports. When he first played the scientific games his greatest hindrance was his inexperience, yet he went into the contest with the determination to win...
>
> "Four years did he struggle having had very little instruction, but for the last three years a skillful architect

> [Warner] has helped him to lay out the same kind of plans as his pale faced brothers have for their athletic foundations. Good fortune befell the Red Man when he secured the services of one who not only presented the usual plans but who improved upon them...
>
> "The Indian is repeating the feats of his ancestors on the race track and has made himself famous as a runner. Not only that but he has made athletic science his warpath thereby making the college world dread him as did their forefathers in old colonial days."

Martin did not return to the reservation after graduating: he stayed at Carlisle for another football season. 1902 was difficult for him as he was laid up much of the time with pleurisy. However, when the faintest opportunity to play presented itself, he was out on the field. That he played at all in the Cornell game is a story of valor that is told best in an article by Pop Warner, excerpts of which are included in Appendix A. Walter Camp didn't award Wheelock even Third Team All America honors this year. *The Philadelphia Inquirer*'s Nathan F. Stauffer explained his reasons for downgrading Wheelock when making his picks:

> "There are three strong candidates for centre position, Holt for several years Yale's pivotal man; Wheelock, the Indian chieftain, and McCabe, the Pennsylvanian. Holt, by his steadiness and his great defensive power, has the place, although the Indian pressed him closely for the honor. The Cornell and Harvard teams gave Wheelock a great deal of credit for stopping many of their attacks. His inability to last a whole game, however, places him second."

If Stauffer had had any idea of the condition in which Wheelock was playing, he would have awarded the Indian stalwart something higher than Second Team accolades.

Martin left Carlisle but didn't abandon football; he joined the 1903 Haskell Institute team in Lawrence, Kansas. Haskell's critics complained about Carlisle players continuing their careers by playing there after exhausting their eligibility at Carlisle. Of course, eligibility rules were just evolving at that time. So, he anchored Haskell's line at left tackle for a year before finishing his college football career.

Now that he was well over a quarter century old, it was time for Martin to put aside the things of childhood and focus on serious pursuits. So, he returned to Wisconsin to farm. On October 18, 1905, he married Lena E. Webster, Oneida, also a former Carlisle student, and they began family life together. Lena had been the third wife, and widow, of James A. Wheelock, father of the famous musicians. Tracing her life was difficult due to, among other things, her being listed as Ellen Wheelock on some censuses while she was married to James. She and Martin farmed on government land at first and raised Lena's two children, in addition to having four together. Martin also practiced the blacksmith trade he learned at Carlisle and eventually farmed his own land. Family legend has it that he played on the independent teams in Green Bay that preceded the formation of the Packers. Already in his 30s, he probably didn't play semi-pro or independent football for very many years.

In 1916, likely as a reaction to the raids conducted by Pancho Villa across the border into the U. S. and the general suspicion of Mexico at the time, Martin joined other former Carlisle and Haskell students in forming a company of soldiers to defend the country from an invasion through the border with Mexico. Six months later, the Zimmerman telegram was intercepted, and Germany's offer to provide Mexico with arms to be used in taking back their former territory was thwarted. So, the offer was not as outlandish as it sounds almost 100 years later.

Lena divorced Martin in 1921, citing cruel and inhuman treatment. He did not contest the divorce. Circuit Court Judge Henry Graass awarded her ten dollars a month alimony for their five children. No property was involved.

Martin Wheelock died in May 1937 at age 65. His obituary listed Lena as his widow. Perhaps the divorce was never finalized or they had later reconciled.

Some years after he had played his last football game, his former coach paid his former lineman a great compliment. In 1913, Pop Warner selected his all-time best Indian players. He chose Wheelock and Wauseka (Emil Hauser) as two members of the team, saying, "Both tackles were magnificent specimens of manhood, and used their brains to advantage."

Other Oneidas

John Webster

Many, if not most, of the boys who attended Carlisle Indian School played on a football team but few of them made the varsity and many who did seldom got to play in games. The intramural system was where most played. Shops, debating clubs, and even the band had teams. Younger boys played on the JV. Superintendent Major Mercer complained about having to outfit fourteen teams every year, only one of which was the varsity squad. Fourteen teams meant plenty of opportunities to play. These teams served as feeders for the varsity. This chapter features photos of Oneidas who didn't play on the varsity.

APPENDICES

A

Toughness

In 1924 J. P. Glass and George Byrnes interviewed Pop Warner for a syndicated column that was distributed nationally by the North American Newspaper Alliance (NANA). In this interview, Warner told of the heroic efforts in 1902 of several past, present and future Carlisle captains: Martin Wheelock, Antonio Lubo, Charles Williams, James Johnson and Albert Exendine, in a big game with Warner's alma mater. This is the story in Warner's own words:

Two men who were dallying with death and should have been in hospital; a third who would have looked well in an invalid's chair; two pieces of leather, which, joined together, closely resembled a puttee; and, finally, a brace of aluminum plate that resembled nothing so much as the rubbing portion of a washboard—these were the chief factors in making possible a strategy that decided one of the most sensational football battles I ever saw.

It was way back in 1902, during my first term of coaching the famous Carlisle Indian team. In those days our annual game with Cornell was one of the biggest events of the season, notwithstanding that during the course of the hectic schedule which the Indians always played we were apt to engage almost every important team in the country. We set a lot of store on winning from the Ithacans, but this year, as the game approached, it looked as if victory was going to be impossible. In earlier games hard luck gave us a kick that sent us reeling, and Saturday, October 18, the day set for our engagement with Cornell, didn't promise to be an occasion for jubilation...

To begin with, my brother Bill had been a big help. Bill was guard at Cornell and one of the best in the game. This year he was captain of the team and mighty anxious to have it make a good showing. Cornell didn't start its training season until September 15 while the Indians got into action on September 1...

I could picture the rest of my brother's thoughts. He stood over six feet one himself and weighed 220 pounds. The Cornell center, Davitt, and the left guard, Hunt, were built in the same proportions. Nobody ever had punctured the Ithacans' lines while those lads were holding forth, but they had done a lot of damage to the other fellows' defense.

So I knew Bill was going back to Cornell to tell his comrades just what he was thinking then: namely, that the Ithacans must keep possession of the ball when they met us a month later and batter our line to pieces. And I had a hunch that the formation he would have in mind for accomplishing this purpose would be their famous guards-back play. In that, you know, one guard got back of the other to carry the ball, with the whole backfield in tandem formation helping them to plow through the enemy's line...

Just then everything went wrong. First, after the initial game of the season, Wheelock, our star left tackle, probably the best man in the position that year and the leading drop and place kicker who did all our booting, was taken sick and sent to the school infirmary. He was thought to have pneumonia, but that was averted and then he had a recurrence of pleurisy from which he had suffered the previous year. His pain was so great that he couldn't bear even to have the bedclothes touch him, and the hospital attendants had to rig up a special apparatus that suspended his sheet above him an inch away that they protected him without coming in contact with his body.

Second, Exendine, our great right end, wrenched his ankle so badly in a succeeding game he could scarcely run.

Third, Schouchuk, who played at center and was as good as there was in the country, was so badly hurt the week before the Cornell game he had to be placed in the hospital.

There I was, with the big battle less than a week away, with a line that my brother Bill had called only "pretty good" completely shot to pieces. What could I do?

Exendine partly solved my troubles. He insisted he would play despite his bad ankle. It was out of the question for him to take his end assignment. We bound his crippled limb with tape so tightly that he couldn't move his foot and shifted him to right tackle, sending Whitely, who played the position regularly, to fill the left tackle place vacated by Wheelock's illness.

But I still had no center and no right end. I could throw in a center that might fill Schouchuk's shoes acceptably, but I could not replace Wheelock, whose kicking would be sadly missed. He was my best offensive weapon, having made at least one field goal in every game he played.

It was at this time that I was given two demonstrations of the red man's courage which fully upheld all the legends of their stoical indifference to suffering ever told. In 1901, when he played the Navy at Annapolis, Lubo, our left tackle, a thin, wiry fellow who made up in bravery and football brains what he lacked in size—he only weighed 160 pounds—had his left wrist smashed and cut open. The injury was slow to heal. We didn't tell him at the time, but the school physician thought he had a tubercular infection. The superintendent of the academy positively refused to let him play any more football. His arm was placed in a sling and he was instructed to indulge in no exercise except walking, and even then he must conserve his strength. Lubo couldn't play, but there was nothing to prevent his watching his team-mates during practice.

Throughout my brother Bill's sojourn, he trudged up and down the field, observing everything that was done, listening to everything that was said. He was a true Indian, talking little but retaining every scrap of information that came his way, although in this case it could be of no value to him.

He was really a pathetic figure. In form, he would have been a tower of strength for us, for despite his size he could hold his own against the huskiest of opponents. But he had been carrying his arm in the sling for a year now and it was shriveled away almost to mere bone.

All the time, though, he was hoping against hope that luck would turn his way. At the start of the season, he applied for permission to play, but the superintendent's only reply was an order to me. "Don't even give him a uniform," he said. "His health means more to the school than winning a couple of football games." Nevertheless he continued his appeals. And when the injury to Schouchuk capped the climax of our troubles he decided to make one more try.

Four nights preceding the Cornell game a knock brought me to my door. There stood Lubo.

"Coach,'" he said without any preliminary, "I'd give anything if I could play against Cornell. I know how Schouchuk and Wheelock can't play. I'd like to go up there for you and for Carlisle."

I brought him inside and explained as gently as I could that it wasn't possible. "Not with that arm," I said.

"But that wouldn't make any difference," he protested.

"I've been exercising and have kept in good shape in every other way. Besides, coach, I think I can do as much with my right arm as with two arms. I can protect my left so it won't get hurt."

I asked where he thought he could play.

"Tackle, in Wheelock's place."

"No. That's out of the question. A tackle must have both arms."

"Well, then, center."

"No, a center must use both hands to pass the ball.'

"Well," he declared. "I know I could play somewhere on the team."

I had to tell him it was impossible, although I appreciated his spirit. But when he left, after two hours of argument, he insisted. "Somehow, I'm going to play."

As to when he saw the superintendent I don't know, for it was half past ten o'clock when he left my house. But the next morning the chief telephoned me to come to his office. Lubo had been to see him again, he said, and had asked to be allowed to face Cornell.

"I told him, no," he added, "but the boy said he must play—he owed it to Carlisle. He's so fine I'm inclined to be lenient, if you and the doctor think it is possible."

I didn't because I believed Lubo would be performing merely on his ambition. But when the physician told me that, except for his left arm, the Indian was in fine condition, I began to change my mind. We could at least let him practice a bit. I told him so the next day, which was the Wednesday preceding the date at Ithaca on Saturday.

He was on hand promptly. It didn't take him long to convince me that, handicapped though he was, he was better than any substitute I could use. If only he hadn't had that withered arm. That night he came around to see me again.

"Coach," he said, "there must be some way to fix my arm."

I thought hard. I've always been handy at repairing injured players and finally hit on a scheme. I dug up two strips of leather. These I sewed around his bad wrist, extending from the tips of his finger to his elbow. We stuffed the inside with cotton and bound the whole in tape. It seemed to offer adequate protection.

"Lubo, it looks like you were going to get into that game," I said.

He just stood there smiling and saying over and over, "Thank you, Coach, thank you."

I don't mind telling you I felt pretty weepy.

Of course Lubo couldn't play end or tackle. I decided to switch Beaver, the right guard, who had done some playing at end, to Exendine's old position and use Lubo in his place. News of this decision soon got me into trouble. All the cripples around the place asked for harness that would enable them to play. But the biggest shock I got came when [Martin] Wheelock showed up at my house. He had been in the infirmary three weeks but in the last few days had been allowed out in the air a bit. Still he was in such pain he couldn't bear to have any one lay a hand on him.

"Now look here, Coach," he said, "if you can fix Lubo you can fix me. There's nothing wrong with my arms or legs; all I've got is pleurisy."

I didn't argue with him. Arguments didn't seem to count much with those Indians. We went up to the engineering school and asked for help. Someone dug up two wide sheets of aluminum, resembling, as I said before, the metal portion of a washboard.

"That's the stuff!" said Wheelock. "First I'll put on a heavy shirt. Then you can fix these on me, one in front and one in back. Bind them with tape, so they won't slip. Put my jersey on over all and I'll be absolutely all right."

There was left but one vacancy on the team. That was center. Fortunately this would be the one position where Wheelock would suffer a minimum of pain, although he was bound to have plenty of it no matter where he was placed. I assigned him to it.

[Warner then discussed some strategy and the events of the game's first half that put Cornell ahead, 6–5.]

The second half got under way with Cornell rushing us off our feet. And yet, just when it seemed that she was about to score, an Indian would appear from nowhere and throw the man carrying the ball for a loss on third down. Mostly it was Lubo and Wheelock. How Lubo did it with his lame arm I don't know. And time after time Wheelock winced in pain as he came in contact with his opponents. But always they are on the job diving over or under interference and bringing down the man with the ball. Williams backed up both. Johnson was wonderful in running back punts. The lame Exendine, at tackle, more than held his own. Well into the second half we got a break which repaid our cripples for their devotion to the team. Williams, standing on Carlisle's 30-yard line, delivered the best punt of the day. It was a wonderful kick that carried the ball a full 50 yards before it touched on Cornell's 30-yard line.

Brewster, the Cornell quarter [back], apparently figured that the ball would roll clear to the line. He decided to let it pass, so that it could be brought out again on the 20-yard line. But after one high bound, the ball took a backward instead of forward leap, and struck the leg of

Martin Wheelock — Antonio Lubo

Tydeman, right end, who had run back to give Brewster interference. This made a free ball of it and Bradley, the Carlisle right end, who had charged down the field, grabbed it.

It was Carlisle's ball on Cornell's 13-yard line, and Quarterback Johnson immediately proceeded to the most brilliant strategy of the game. This consisted in using the same formation, with variations, four times in succession... [Warner then described an early incarnation of his single-wingback formation which was designed to protect his crippled players. Johnson's brilliant strategy used fakes, deception and speed to confuse the defense as to where the ball was going and who was carrying it. On the fourth play of the series, Willliams dove over the middle of the line for the go ahead touchdown.]

Lubo was able to continue after this play, but Wheelock's outraged body could endure no more. He fell in an agony of pain and had to be taken from the field. This necessitated the only substitution of the game. We missed the goal after touchdown and the score was Carlisle 10; Cornell, 6.

But the game was won. Williams played center on defense and we held the Ithacans until the whistle blew. Was Lubo happy? Was he! And that reminds me. After the game that night I talked again with Bill, my brother.

"How did Lubo impress you, Bill?" I asked.

"Say, Glenn, was that fellow in uniform when I was down at Carlisle?"

"No, he's the one who followed you around with his arm in a sling watching you at practice."

"Well, if that fellow can play like that when he's crippled," replied Bill, "I'd hate to tackle him when he was in good condition."

In view of the fact that Bill was placed on the All-American that year by Walter Camp and all the other critics, his performance in the Carlisle game being praised particularly, I consider he paid Lubo a fine tribute. But the boy deserved everything good that could be said about him.

And Wheelock, too. The strategy by which Johnson won the game was fine; but never so wonderful as the splendid feat of these two boys in playing that day. When you get down to facts, it was their devotion to their school and their team that beat Cornell. There's a lesson in it for every lad that aspires to play the game.

CARLISLE STRATEGY WHICH WON GAME

Glenn Warner and the story he tells illustrated by a diagram prepared by George Byrnes of the Colgate football department.

KEY TO THE PLAY—A (Johnson, Carlisle quarter) received ball from center and, faking end run, sped to right. B (Williams, Carlisle fullback) who on previous formations had faked line plunge, took ball from Johnson. C (Carlisle right halfback) and D (Carlisle left halfback) ran to right as though to protect A (Quarterback Johnson). With latter drawing attention of Cornell backs, B (Williams) made flying dive over Cornell line, just too quick for a Cornell back to stop him, and scored the winning touchdown.

B
Players with Years Played

Identifying all the players who at one time were on the varsity squad, including Second and Third Teams, Reserves, and Scrubs, was a difficult task. The Carlisle student files were incomplete, newspaper accounts were inaccurate, and no one who was alive at that time was available to consult. The likelihood that some of the information that follows is inaccurate is high in spite of the author doing everything he could do to ensure completeness and accuracy.

Archiquette, Chauncey (Oneida)	1896	1897	1898	1905
Baird, Charles (Oneida)	1915			
Charles, Wilson (Oneida)	1900	1901	1902	1903
	1904	1905	1906	
Cornelius, Casper (Oneida)	1906			
Cornelius, Joel (Oneida)	1898	1900	1902	
Cornelius, Phillip (Oneida)	1908	1909	1911	1912
Cornelius, Sampson (Oneida)	1900			
Denny, Wallace (Oneida)	1903	1904	1905	
Doxtator, Benjamin (Oneida)	1893			
George, David (Oneida)	1912			
Hill, Levi E. (Oneida)	1909			
Island, Louis (Oneida)	1906	1907	1910	
Metoxen, Emerson (Oneida)	1917			
Metoxen, James (Oneida)	1904			
Metoxen, Jonas (Oneida)	1893	1894	1895	1896
	1897	1898	1899	
Moore, Job J. (Oneida)	1903			
Reed, Amos (Oneida)	1896			
Sickles, Caleb (Oneida)	1898	1899		
Skenandore, Benjamin (Oneida)	1913	1914		
Skenandore, Fred (Oneida)	1912	1913	1914	
Skenandore, Thomas A. (Oneida)	1894	1895		
Webster, Lewis (Oneida)	1898			
Wheelock, Hugh (Oneida)	1907	1908	1909	1910
	1911			
Wheelock, Joel (Oneida)	1908	1909	1910	1911
	1912			
Wheelock, Martin (Oneida)	1893	1894	1895	1896
	1897	1898	1899	1900
	1901	1902		

Illustrations

Cover
Artwork created by Lone Star Dietz for 1909 Athletic Banquet frontispiece.

Frontispiece
Grayscale version of drawing done by Lone Star Dietz for 1909 Athletic Banquet frontispiece.

Headpiece
Grayscale version of artwork created by Lone Star Dietz for cover of *Football for Players and Coaches* by Glenn S. Warner, 1912.

Introduction
Photo courtesy of National Anthropological Archives, Smithsonian Institution.
Pratt with student photo courtesy of U. S. Army Military History Institute, Carlisle, PA.

Chapter 1 Charles Archiquette
Photo of Archiquette, Roy & Guyon courtesy of Cecilia Balenti-Moddelmog.

Chapter 2 Charles Baird
Photo of nurses in front of Model T ambulance courtesy of Ford Media.
Hunka Tin poem from American Field Service Bulletin.

Chapter 3 Wilson Charles
Wilson Charles Sr. photo courtesy of Barb Skenandore.
Photo of Elizabeth Knudsen courtesy of U. S. Army Military History Institute.
Buster Charles photo courtesy of Barb Skenandore.

Chapter 4 Casper Cornelius
Photo of Oxford Indian baseball team courtesy of History Nebraska.

Chapter 5 Joel Cornelius
Photo of Joel Cornelius courtesy of Cumberland County Historical Society.

Chapter 6 Phillip Cornelius

Chapter 7 Sampson Cornelius

Chapter 8 Wallace Denny
Photo of Wallace Denny as a student courtesy of Cumberland County Historical Society.
Photo of "Dr." Denny with sweatbox courtesy of U. S. Army Military History Institute.
Photo of Denny visiting his family courtesy of U. S. Army Military History Institute.
Photo of Nelie V. Robertson courtesy of Cumberland County Historical Society.
Photo of Denny family courtesy of U. S. Army Military History Institute.
Photo of Wallace Denny with tennis racquet courtesy of U. S. Army Military History Institute.

Chapter 9 Benjamin Doxtator
Photo of Benjamin Doxtator courtesy of Cumberland County Historical Society.

Chapter 10 David George

Chapter 11 Levi E. Hill/Hillman
Class of 1910 photo courtesy of Cumberland County Historical Society.

Chapter 12 Louis Island
Photo of Louis Island in WWI uniform courtesy of Iris Davis.
Graduation photo of Louis Island courtesy of Louis Geoffrey Johnston.
Photo of Louis & Phoebe Island courtesy of Louis Geoffrey Johnston.

Chapter 13 Emerson Metoxen
1917 football team photo courtesy of U. S. Army Military History Institute.
1918 lacrosse team photo courtesy of *Harrisburg Telegraph*.
Imperator photo courtesy of NavSource Naval History.
YCI photo courtesy of York College of Pennsylvania.
LVC team photo courtesy of *Sunday News*, Lancaster, Pennsylvania.

Chapter 14 James Metoxen

Chapter 15 Jonas Metoxen
Jonas Metoxen sketch courtesy of Wire Service.
1900 team photo courtesy of Cumberland County Historical Society.
Jonas Metoxen photo courtesy of Cumberland County Historical Society.

Chapter 16 Job J. Moore
Cynthia Webster photo courtesy of Cumberland County Historical Society.
1903 team photo courtesy of *1904 Spaulding's Guide*.

Chapter 17 Amos Reed
Team lineups courtesy of *Stevens Point Journal*.
Katie Metoxen photo courtesy of National Anthropological Archives, Smithsonian Institution.

Chapter 18 Caleb Sickles
Photo of Caleb Sickles with his mother courtesy of Justine Souto.
Photo of Sickles' home courtesy of *The Red Man October 1910*.
Photo of Dr. Sickles at work courtesy of *The Red Man October 1910*.

Chapter 19 Benjamin Skenandore

Chapter 20 Fred Skenandore

Chapter 21 Thomas Skenandore
Green Bay Gridders clipping courtesy of *Breen Bay Press Gazette*.
Photo of Zippa Metoxen Skenandore's daughters courtesy of National Archives.

Chapter 22 Lewis Webster
Webster siblings photo courtesy of Cumberland County Historical Society.

Chapter 23 Hugh & Joel Wheelock
Joel Wheelock photo courtesy of Fred Wardecker.
Hugh Wheelock photo courtesy of U. S. Army Military History Institute.
Joel Wheelock in track uniform courtesy of Cumberland County Historical Society.
Wheelock's Indian Band photo courtesy of www.sousaontherez.com.

Chapter 24 Martin Wheelock
1898 team photo courtesy of U. S. Army Military History Institute.

Chapter 25 Other Oneidas
Photo of John Webster courtesy of Barb Skenandore.
Photos of Joel Moore and Taylor Smith courtesy of Barb Skenandore.

Appendix A

Martin Wheelock photo courtesy of U. S. Army Military History Institute.
Antonio Lubo photo courtesy of U. S. Army Military History Institute.
Carlisle Strategy courtesy of *The Des Moines Register,* October 26, 1924.

www.ingramcontent.com/pod-product-compliance
Lightning Source LLC
Chambersburg PA
CBHW070054080526
44586CB00013B/1049